# Praise for *Attract or Repel*

"Walt has written a great book on how to measure organizational Trust, Courage and Employee Engagement. If measurable organizational health is important to you, this is *the* book to read."

—*Gino Wickman, author of* Traction *and* The EOS Life

"I want to highlight Gino Wickman's endorsement of this book. Gino is the master of simplifying that which is complex, getting to the root of the issue. His endorsement is a nod to Walt creating something that is simple, measurable, and actionable.

"Businesses are naturally complex and, as you grow and add people, it becomes exponentially more complicated as each individual brings their own flavor to your culture. In *Attract or Repel*, Walt has simplified that complexity by providing a simple recipe to mix and harmonize all the flavors. It is the Seven Critical Needs and BITE Framework that any entrepreneurial leader can use to make their organization more efficient, effective, and enjoyable!"

—*Joe Paulsen, Expert EOS Implementer*

"A fantastic read with philosophical commonsense advice and practical approaches and tools to inject a high level of employee engagement, trust, buy-in, and courage—a true competitive advantage in your company.

"When everyone knows how and why we are measuring something, we can work on it, improve it together. Now we have a way to measure organizational trust, courage, and engagement, and we can work on it."

—*Alex Freytag, coauthor of* Profit Works *and Expert EOS Implementer*

"I was 28 when Walt helped transform my career, and ultimately my life as we worked together to discover the Seven Questions. His approach through the Seven Promises, his mastery of how they tie to the EOS BOS model and knowledge of how humans work, along with his coaching, is unmatched. Walt believed in me and gave me the tools to believe even when I may not have believed in myself. I discovered fearlessness and bravery, Courage on this journey with Walt, and I am truly grateful for his friendship. The approach works and is scalable."

—*Client, Kerrie Lang, millennial integrator of Thornton Brothers Inc.*

"I *loved Attract or Repel*. It is succinct, laden with insight, and readily applicable. Every entrepreneur should take the Seven Critical Needs Survey and work toward improving their BITE. It will be transformative for you and your company."

—*Jonathan B. Smith, author of* Optimize for Growth *and Expert EOS Implementer*

"Walt has an incredible ability to connect with his clients in a very simple and authentic manner to get things done. I had run a company for over 10 years before first working with Walt. I wish we had met earlier. In *Attract or Repel*, he has done it again and has put into words and action the 'lessons learned.' Every organization should be making sure that their people have clear answers to the 'Seven'—a book that will produce value when read over and over again. Thanks, Walt."

—*Client, Austin Koon, Davis Moore Capital*

"Walt gets right at the root of many organizations' struggles—people issues. It is critical to attract individuals who embody a company's core values and to repel those who would hamper the organization's success. Once you find and hire those superstars, keeping them engaged and productive is just as important as finding them. The Seven Critical Needs provide an excellent framework for tracking employee engagement. Overall, *Attract or Repel* provides a formula for scaling your business by the right people for exponential growth."

—*Alec Broadfoot, CEO, Vision Spark*

"This book is so good! The first thing I thought of is how critical it is for a company that wants to succeed to do this. Becoming a "courageous organization" is critical to success for any company looking to thrive. It changed the way we think and act and is a major catalyst in our company."

—*Client, Mercer F. Stanfield, president and COO, Brame*

"It is impossible to quantify how valuable Walt Brown and his teachings have been to McGreat LLC (dba Great Clips franchisee) and its owners. Of course, there are the numbers: Since implementing EOS, McGreat and its affiliates have expanded our holdings from 16 to 47 Great Clips stores, increased revenues by millions of dollars, and even gotten into another franchised concept. Those numbers are easy to recite, but they only tell half the story. The rest of the story is more difficult to quantify because it involves taking the time to understand the value you place on your own emotional health as a business owner. What value would you place on feeling like your business was focused on the right problems, hiring the right people, and growing in the right direction? How much would it be worth to you to feel like your business is operating under a set of timeless and repeatable principles that develop your leaders and allow you the freedom and flexibility to enjoy your life on your terms? Quantify the value of those feelings and then, and only then, will you have your answer as to what Walt, the Seven Promises, and EOS have meant to McGreat.

"If you aren't running a business operating system that answers the Seven Critical Needs and are just winging it with effort and talent, then I truly feel sorry for you. Not because I think you are stupid, but because I have been there before. Can you imagine an NFL team trying to win games or score a touchdown by drawing plays in the dirt? Yet that is exactly how most people choose to run their business. They just make it up as they go along because that is how it has always been. As an organization grows, it needs a system. To get to positive alignment on the Seven Critical Needs, it needs core values, a plan, and plays it can run on a weekly and daily basis so it can grow. Walt can give your team the complete BITE playbook. He gives you a system and teaches you how to run winning plays. So, drop your stick, quit drawing up your business plan in the dirt, and get busy growing in the right direction. Your team and family will thank you."
—*Client, James Cummings and Pat McLaughlin, co-CEOs of McGreat LLC*

"Such a deep discovery, these Seven Critical Needs. And I really am impressed with your use of the word *courageous* . . . it's almost the manifestation of self- actualization. Really describes why EOS works."
—*Jill Young, Honey Badger, head implementer coach,*
*Expert EOS Implementer, and author of* Earn It!

"Great insights, wisdom, and a lot to learn. It was chewy and made me think. (Note: if you get the Seven Promises, you will get the message. Simple.) Walt is a wise man with great insight."
—*Sue Hawkes, CEO of YESS! and fellow Honey Badger*

"Walt presented the Seven Critical Needs to our group on our first retreat and completely transformed the culture with this process. As the founder of the company, I want everyone to have the same passion as I do about my business. And by getting my staff to *yes* on Walt's Seven Critical Needs, I am now able to develop my staff and have them see their careers within this business while becoming extremely passionate, engaged, and courageous."
—*Client, Dr. Austin Cohen, founder of Corrective Chiropractic*

"Incredibly insightful and a critical read for anyone wanting to, or struggling with, engaging their employees. The best short book on this topic since *The Great Game of Business* and *Ownership Thinking*."
—*Tom Bouwer, author of* What the Heck Is EOS, *international keynote speaker, leadership team coach—Pinnacle*

"This is an exciting and much needed contribution from the trenches. Brown has simplified and condensed decades of his pioneering work building courageous organizations to Seven Critical Needs your team members will answer. This dynamic approach can eliminate dysfunction while achieving significant organizational loyalty and improvement. The results speak for themselves. *Ya gotta read this book!!*"

—*Greg Walker, coach to over 300 business owners for more than 30 years*

"What I like best about this is that it's full of what I call 'Waltisms.' As integrator at Counter Culture, I rely heavily not only on EOS but on the lessons peppered in the EOS coaching from Walt. I recite them often as Waltisms—nuggets of wisdom or thought-provoking questions that help drive an organization's implementation of a BOS.

"*Attract or Repel* complements EOS well because it helps further define the connection a leader and a company have with the most important (in my opinion) key function of EOS: people.

"The concept of EATT is also really important. Much more concise than *Five Dysfunctions* and logically connects trust to actions: trying, adapting, evolving. It's a powerful reminder of the value and necessity of trust.

"Lastly, and man this one kinda blew my mind, I really like the idea that a company is essentially a fiction, given power by people believing in it. I love it."

—*Client, Brian Ludviksen, integrator at Counter Culture Coffee*

"If you want a business book that gives you the right questions to ask instead of empty answers that may or may not serve your needs, this is the book. This is the business book if you want a tangible tool to address today's most challenging business issues (and have a few good giggles)."

—*Sara B. Stern, author of* Start Here: A Guide to Family Business Succession *and* Married to the Family Business: A Handbook for Spouses of Family Business Owners

"Walt Brown's *Attract or Repel* masterfully distills decades of experience into actionable insights for building high-trust, agreements-based cultures. In this book, Walt provides a simple yet powerful framework that ensures leaders attract the right people and repel the wrong ones. For anyone committed to creating a thriving, courageous organization, this is an indispensable guide. I've known Walt for over a decade, and we are deeply aligned in our belief that trust and clear agreements are the foundation of great company cultures."

—*Mark Abbott, founder and CEO of Ninety, Inc.*

# ATTRACT

## OR

# REPEL

**Also by Walt Brown**

*The Patient Organization: Attracting, Engaging,
and Empowering Team Players*

*Death of the Org Chart, Rise of the Organizational Graph*

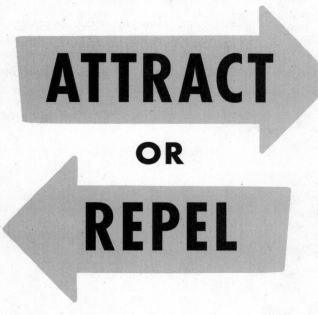

# ATTRACT
## OR
# REPEL

### SEVEN KEYS TO
Magnetize Your Company and Build
the Culture of Your Dreams

**WALT BROWN**

BenBella Books, Inc.
Dallas, TX

BenBella Books, Inc.
8080 N. Central Expressway
Suite 1700
Dallas, TX 75206
benbellabooks.com
Send feedback to feedback@benbellabooks.com

*BenBella* is a federally registered trademark.

Printed in the United States of America
10 9 8 7 6 5 4 3 2 1

Library of Congress Control Number: 2024034200
ISBN 9781637746158 (hardcover)
ISBN 9781637746165 (electronic)

Editing by Camille Cline
Copyediting by Scott Calamar
Proofreading by Denise Pangia and Marissa Wold Uhrina
Text design and composition by PerfecType, Nashville, TN
Interior illustrations by Rogelio Hernandez G.
Cover design by Sarah Avinger
Cover art (arrows) by Rogelio Hernandez G.
Printed by Lake Book Manufacturing

*To my wife, Anne, the ultimate pragmatist, who has kept*
*my thoughts grounded for more than 40 years.*
*To my father and patient mentor, Walter Jr., who loved to hear me say,*
*"Guess what?" because what came after that was always a zinger.*

# CONTENTS

# FOREWORD

**IT WAS EIGHT** short years ago that I'd been hired as the Integrator and President of EOS Worldwide. What I knew at the time is that EOS, the Entrepreneurial Operating System, is a simple set of concepts and practical tools that helps thousands of entrepreneurs around the world get what they want from their business. What I also knew is that EOS Implementers are the best of the best at teaching, facilitating, and coaching entrepreneurs and their teams, serving as the cornerstone of coaching for small to midsized companies running on EOS.

My first priority in my new seat was to attend and experience a 100-person EOS event filled with EOS Implementers. What I could not fully appreciate at the time is that the EOS Implementer community has within its cultural DNA, dating back to our founders Gino Wickman and Don Tinney, a very special, abundance-minded, help-first approach to helping one another and the world at large. It's palpable in any room where implementers are present. And it's immeasurable in that it makes people feel and engage together in the healthiest way, which has transformed 230,000 companies globally. The event felt truly electric, exceeding my expectations, as it was even better than it had been described to me in advance.

With such a massive number of gifted individuals and energy in one room, it's hard to imagine, yet there was one person within the crowd who stood out to me. This guy with such humor, intelligence, and enthusiasm bounding around the room, connecting with everyone in ways that exhibit a mastery of understanding, and authentically loving, and caring for people. That one person was Walt Brown.

A lot has happened since that time, as Walt and I ultimately forged a unique and deep friendship and respect for one another. It's born out of our shared belief around building a courageously patient organization with an intentional culture. What I've learned from Walt, and what you can expect to learn in the pages of *Attract or Repel*, is this reality: "the answer is in the tools."

When you combine a turnkey business operating system, or BOS, with the BITE7 survey and BITE Index report (representing buy-in, inclusion, trust, and engagement), entrepreneurs, owners, leaders, and managers achieve the highest possible commitment for, and with, their entire team. This is how organizations get serious about building healthy, cohesive teams where these Seven Promises prevail: *belonging* based on core values; *belief* in the strategic direction; *accountability* for results that are *measured*; feeling *heard*, valued, and appreciated; opportunities to be *developed*; and last, but definitely not least, an ability to live a *balanced* life. At EOS, we call this the EOS Life: doing what you love, with people you love, making a huge difference, being compensated appropriately, with time for other passions.

While it takes much courage, patience, grit, and determination to create a place where all these things are true, the rewards and benefits are extraordinary. You will find yourself attracting and retaining the right-fit teammates who deliver on your company promises. You will get optimum clarity for who to hire; and you're no longer struggling to articulate to potential candidates who you are, what you do, and what your company represents in the world. Members of your team who are not the right fit begin to self-select out of your company because of this clarity you've created. You have achieved alignment within your team top to bottom. There is a very high level of foundational trust established among the team who has observed your promises honored in your words, actions, and behaviors. Suddenly a line of people who can't wait to be part of an organization that cares enough to make these Seven Promises—and keep them—builds.

In the 25 years I've had the honor and privilege of serving entrepreneurial companies, there is one truth that remains: If you put people first, the rest of the issues take care of themselves. Over and over again I've witnessed it: how genuine, intentional development of, and care for, individuals and teams is the most unifying thing any organization can do. This is where the magic lives.

A key tenet we hold true at EOS is that as goes the Visionary/ Integrator relationship (those at the helm of every entrepreneurial company) so goes the leadership team. And as the leadership team goes, so goes the rest of the entire organization. The pattern required for leading and serving well is not for the faint of heart. And yet, the simple, practical tools used in organizational operating systems paired with Walt's framework for BITE7 Seven Questions Survey, comparative index, and Seven Promises creates a really solid, reliable road map. If only all leaders and managers everywhere could embrace these disciplines and tools to make their dreams a reality, what a world this would be!

My encouragement for you is to trust the process Walt describes within these pages, lean in on the tools outlined, and bring your very best intentions to the table. Commit and have the courage required to do the work. With that, Walt's words of wisdom provide all you need to measure your organization's health and systematize how you achieve the healthiest culture that delivers on your organization's purpose, cause, passion, or mission. And then, and only then, will you have created the opening for the best possible team collaboration and break through to 10X growth.

May you enjoy the people-focused journey ahead of you and navigate successfully to *Attract or Repel*.

Kelly Knight
President and Integrator, EOS Worldwide
Author, *People: Dare to Build an Intentional Culture*
(EOS Mastery Collection)

# INTRODUCTION

**CONSIDER THE PROMISES** you made to yourself when you took the risk to lead your organization. You promised yourself you were going to create an amazing place to work, the workplace you always dreamed of. But, somewhere along the line, you started breaking those promises to yourself and have created something that is unremarkable, a mess, or worse yet, a nightmare. It is time to flip that script by making a new set of promises that you will keep.

You may be allowing people who do not buy in to hang around and destroy your company culture and its future. If someone on your team will not agree to the mission, core values, and guiding principles of the organization, then that person may derail efforts to solve challenges, ultimately holding the organization back. They must be repelled. Or perhaps your organization is not as healthy as it could be. You are leaving tons of money and opportunity on the table by not being brave enough or methodical enough to clean up your own house, your own organization.

My goal is to help you permanently install a systematic approach that *attracts* great people and *repels* the bad ones. You have no room for and cannot afford detractors.

Even when you have installed a "turnkey" BOS (business operating system), such as EOS or Pinnacle or Scaling Up or 4DX or System & Soul, there is still plenty of efficiency and opportunity to be harvested. Having invested in a BOS is a good start. Now use it to create *robust, measurable organizational health.*

You can easily measure the effectiveness of your BOS and audit its ability to attain and maintain robust organizational health by focusing on Seven Critical Needs and then scoring how you stack up to the rest of the world via the BITE Index (buy-in, inclusion, trust, engagement).

The BITE Index measures organizational health, and it measures the strength and effectiveness of your BOS to make and keep Seven Promises—the promises that answer each member of your team's Seven Critical Needs. The Seven Promises are the bedrock of robust organizational health. Your BITE Index is your barometer and road map; it will show you where to put in the effort on your way to attaining and maintaining robust organizational health.

Through my years of leading successful companies and working with focused teams and collaborative clients, I have discovered that these Seven Critical Needs comprise to *belong*, to *believe*, to be *accountable*, to be *measured*, to be *heard*, to be *developed*, and to be *balanced*.

The work starts with an initial BITE Survey and BITE Index report. Using this feedback, your leadership team and you must buckle down and define what a positive response to each of the Seven Critical Needs looks like from the organization's standpoint. Then you ask, "Does my BOS have the tools to allow my people to participate in attaining and maintaining a positive response inside each of the Seven Critical Needs?"

Distinguished 17th-century architect Sir Christopher Wren shared a story about buy-in, inclusion, trust, and employee engagement. Yes, there was interest in employee engagement in the year 1678.

Wren, who was highly regarded for designing many of London's finest churches, was visiting the job site of his St. Paul's Cathedral project in London.

His visit took him to the stonemason's pit.

He came upon a mason and asked, "What are you doing?"

The worker answered, "I am cutting these stones to a certain size and shape."

He asked the same question of a second worker, and the worker answered, "I am cutting stones for a certain wage."

He came to a third mason and asked the question again. This time the worker got up from his work, straightened himself, and replied, "I am helping Sir Christopher Wren build St. Paul's Cathedral."

This story is exactly the kind of buy-in my team and I try to help our clients create. We want their folks—and yours—to stand tall and say, "I am helping John build the best company he can. I am not anonymous or irrelevant."

How did we get here? In a typical year my team and I each get to spend eight hours a day across 130 days huddled with the senior leadership teams of 25 different companies doing the gutsy work of improving their organizations. Organizations are comprised of people and, through the years, we noticed that complaints by people and about people often included the millennial- and Gen Z-stereotype excuse.

This confused us. Every week we worked with millennials who are part of our senior teams and are not only smart, engaged, and hard-working, but also poised to take over the world. Why the disconnect? The teams and organizations we worked with did not share a bias against millennials or Gen Z workers. What was it that we were doing together that was breaking this stereotype?

We started having discussions with them, trading thoughts and emails, looking for the pattern, probing for what made them different, what was breaking the mold. With our millennials and Gen Z colleagues, we distilled their feedback down to a clear pattern that led to the discovery of the Seven Critical Needs. These critical needs distinguished companies that were happy with their younger staff—and, ultimately, all their employees—from those that were not.

As we refined the Seven Critical Needs and shared them with everyone from programmers, receptionists, and salespeople to CEOs and business owners, we realized that we had discovered not just needs but jewels. In each study, everyone felt that we were getting at all the things that motivated and engaged them at work. It did not seem possible to hit all the areas that would satisfy, inspire, and empower team members with just seven, but as we looked for an eighth, people told us again and again that we had covered all the bases with the seven.

It's simple. When we presented them in the form of promises, we realized that when leaders could get all team members to align positively in these seven areas, most of the complaints disappeared. The dysfunction faded, and the organization enjoyed the kind of advantages that left competitors dazed.

We continued testing the Seven Critical Needs thesis. As team coaches, we have worked with industrial rigging and construction companies, IT and software companies, for-profit health care businesses, a nonprofit battling homelessness, a boutique real estate brokerage, a local SPCA branch, Oak Ridge and Sandia National Laboratories—the national research labs—a coffee company, a hair salon franchise, and many more. The seven worked for all of them—enormous, tiny, for profit, nonprofit. If your organization has people, the seven apply, and this book is for you.

This is not to say that getting to positive alignment is easy. On the contrary, it's difficult, takes time, and often causes pain. My goal in this book is to make alignment as smooth as possible.

This is something my team and I are doing *with and for* our people, not *to* them. Our great people do not want to be surrounded by a bunch of coworkers who do not buy in. Via the Seven Critical Needs, the BITE Survey, the BITE Index, and your BOS, you empower your people to help you attract and repel on your way to attaining and maintaining robust, measurable organizational health.

## Attaining and Maintaining Positive Alignment

The Seven Critical Needs and the promises they led to explained how and why the things we did as team coaches—and that we had done running our own companies—worked. Let me back up here and explain briefly how we came to work as coaches for the clients we call PBOLTs—private business owners with *leadership teams* (pronounced P-Bolt). I always dreamed of building my own company, and for this I knew I needed to build perspective, knowledge, and experience as fast as I could. In school, I studied business, accounting, and statistics. (Ironically, I am a dyslexic numbers guy.) Straight out of school, I worked for the "big eight" CPA firm, EY (Ernst & Whinney, then, before its merger with Arthur Young & Co.), for four audit seasons—this was my strategy to build the knowledge and perspective I cited above.

In 1986, I went into the mail order catalog business, selling stuff to households that included someone who raced sailboats. Readers of a certain age will remember that at the time, the Lands' End clothes catalog appeared poised to take over the world. My catalog ideas grew into Layline (a sailing term), which became a dot-com, and expanded into equestrian-related goods—on the premise that where there's smoke there's fire, and where there's a sailboat there's probably a horse.

Through the catalog, we became good at finding European brands that wanted a foothold in the United States. We would set up the company here and create distribution for them and then basically sell the business back to the brand. After years of doing that successfully, we captured the attention of a family office that inquired about buying the business in 2006.

I was on the board of Sail America, our trade association, at the time, and before I sold my company, I attended a board meeting where George Day, the guy who ran *SAIL* magazine, held forth about the coach who helped with his strategic thinking and the peer board he relied on for consulting. I loved the idea and was grilling him about it when light bulbs went off around the table. "You'd be great at that, Walt," was the consensus of the board.

George told me all about TAB, The Alternative Board, and soon after, I bought the franchise for the Raleigh-Durham area. A month after selling Layline Inc., the mother ship and her three sub-brands, I had 48 TAB clients. I had success getting business owners on board with the TAB approach, which involves aligning personal vision with business vision, as well as following a strategic thinking method called "critical success factor."

Nine months later, pleased TAB clients were saying that they knew where they wanted to go with their lives and businesses. Could I come in to meet with their leadership team to help them pivot and turn the ship to get there? My own companies had been courageous, nimble, and strategic, so I didn't hesitate to say yes.

I went to six appointments with teams and presented this business-school approach to strategic planning. At first, everyone around the table seemed to be thinking, *this will be great*. By the time I was halfway through the sessions, though, they were staring at the ceiling, tongues lolling, clearly thinking, *Oh no, another strategic planning retreat that's going nowhere*. Their frustration was palpable.

I did not have a concrete, strategic way to help my clients turn the ship, it turned out. I had made those pivots in my businesses numerous times, but I couldn't coach someone else on how to do it. It was the story of the great athlete who is unable to coach others to do what they do—they can't explain it. I called my clients and told them I did not yet have a way to help them execute their vision but that I knew one was out there and I was determined to find it.

I dug in and read all the business books making waves then: *Good to Great, Built to Last, How the Best Get Better, The Five Dysfunctions of a*

*Team, The E-Myth, In Search of Excellence.* My reactions ran the gamut. I learned a lot, but even the authors with valuable ideas were writing what I call 20,000-foot books. They all had views from an altitude of 20,000 feet, which looked beautiful, but no one was explaining how to make their vision happen on the ground.

Miraculously, Don Tinney and the Entrepreneurial Operating System discovered me, and once Don laid out the EOS Model and its tools to me, I thought without hesitation: *Here it is. There is no need to look any further.* EOS gets to the heart of the mechanics of what I did best in my businesses but couldn't communicate to my TAB clients. I knew in my gut that EOS provided business leaders with a key first step, an implementable business operating system. I brought the system back to the half dozen clients I'd put on hold and then ran another 27 through an EOS implementation over the next 18 months. The results were so good I sold my TAB practice to my partner, Keith Weaver, and hung my shingle as a focused EOS Implementer. I was the third EOS Implementer, and now, in addition to creating courageously patient organizations with BITE, I continue practicing as an Expert EOS Implementer. Also, I am now the coach of 84 Expert EOS Implementers at EOS Worldwide.

I will explore EOS, AKA Traction, and other business "organizational operating systems" in more detail in part II, but briefly, a good business operating system provides an efficient way for businesses to clarify exactly who is responsible for what and to focus the company's vision: why it exists, what it does, where it's going.

## A Brief Note About Business Operating Systems

A business operating system allows an organization to codify how it functions. A concrete set of BOS tools helps owners set priorities, review team members, track numbers, develop marketing strategies, and communicate. I've used EOS to help transform the cultures and boost the bottom lines of more than 200 companies at press time, and our coaches have helped thousands.

Having the perspective of growing and running four companies of my own, I was smitten by the EOS Model and its results but could never fully explain why it worked so well. Over time, we made yet another discovery: business operating systems work because they are how we keep our Seven Promises, how we maintain positive alignment to the Seven Critical Needs. The tools of a BOS must help an organization maintain positive alignment to the Seven Critical Needs, and the best business operating systems leave no gaps.

It is the opposite of the intangible business-school strategizing that caused my TAB clients' eyes to glaze over during my first ill-fated attempts to help them execute their vision. Business operating systems are implemented and run at ground level, not 20,000 feet up. They are concrete, not theoretical.

A company must have a BOS—whether it's developed organically, ad hoc (as mine were, when I ran Layline), or imported, with clearly articulated tools, like EOS, 4DX, Rockefeller Habits, Scaling Up, Pinnacle, Holacracy, and others. Without one, leaders find themselves running from fire to fire, and strategic thinking suffers. Accountability, metrics, purpose—all the keys to running a successful organization—suffer because clarity, structure, and reliable processes are in short supply.

In my view, a business operating system's purpose is to build buy-in, inclusion, trust, and engagement into the organization so that workers have the courage and patience to do their best work and share their ideas, empowering and equipping them to respond rather than react. Both involve taking action as a result of new developments or information, but reacting is defensive, rushed, uncontrolled, survival oriented, and often emotional. Responding is logical, thoughtful, data based, and goal oriented.

In the early part of the last decade and a half, as I helped transform the culture of businesses through my EOS work, I kept trying to understand exactly why EOS works so well. This question was a constant companion running alongside my quest to understand what millennials and Gen Z colleagues want at work. The answer to both questions was the same, we realized in the end: the Seven Critical Needs. The seven key things that inspire young people—and all workers—are also the hidden principles on which EOS and a few other business operating systems rest.

The tools of a good BOS must help a company maintain positive alignment on the seven. If the system doesn't address and maintain positive alignment on all seven, the gaps eventually spell trouble for any business relying on it. I realize that the relationship between the two can sound a little circular, but I hope that it appears more and more symbiotic later in the book, as we explore the Seven Critical Needs and Promises in depth, and as I offer practical direction regarding what to look for in a BOS to help you get positive alignment.

## What's Inside

In part I, we begin with some of the theory that underlies organizational life, business operating systems, and our views of BITE, courage, patience, leadership, and dysfunction. It is shorter because it is primarily theoretical, and this is not a primarily theoretical book. But part I is not all theory; it is also intended to be extremely practical and hands-on, with concrete steps you can begin using tomorrow. In part II, we'll roll up our sleeves to see how and why the seven work, identify the obstacles to avoid, and supply a diagnostic to see how far from positive alignment your organization is on each of the seven. I will help you understand how to get to the first positive alignment and what to look for in a BOS to help you maintain positive alignment.

Lee Walker, the millennial CEO of Walker Auto & Truck, who you will meet throughout this book, says, "When we flip the script and turn the Seven Critical Needs into Seven Promises, we create a powerful tool for communicating our core values, providing direction, and engaging workers.

"We talk about the Seven Promises openly, and it's part of our EOS presentation," Walker says, referencing one of the business operating systems we'll discuss in part II. "I stand up in front of everybody and tell them it's my job to lead an organization where there's a high degree of belonging, which is based on shared belief and a common understanding of who we are as a company and what we're trying to do. We want to create a place where people understand and embrace what they're accountable for, which comes with a commitment from the company to create great ways to measure what we do. We have ears to listen, so speak up. We're excited about you leaning in and being able to self-develop and, ultimately, to achieve balance."

According to another popular legend, during a tour of NASA headquarters in 1961, John F. Kennedy encountered a janitor mopping the floors.

"Why are you working so late?" Kennedy asked.

"Mr. President," the janitor responded, "I'm helping put a man on the moon."

Putting a man on the moon requires buy-in from every person in the organization.

The one thing that cannot be instantly copied is engaged employees with BITE. You know who they are. They are your folks who believe in your vision, assume accountability, live in a productive reasoning mode, are not fearful and defensive, who stand up, hold their shoulders back, and say, "I am part of the team, and we are doing this."

We train owners and leaders in the use of tools that allow them to consistently hire and motivate employees who stand tall and think of their work as more than their job. They are teammates on a team driving to a common vision, a common goal.

# PART
# ONE

# Defining a Courageously Patient Organization with BITE

# CHAPTER 1

# The Backstory

**MOST ORGANIZATIONS BEGIN** with a dream. Someone is passionate about a product, service, or cause, and, at some point, they realize they can provide it better or faster or cheaper than the next guy. Founders take on the considerable risk of starting businesses because they know they are good at this thing, whatever it is, and they have a vision for an organization, a dream. Most worked for others before striking out on their own and were dissatisfied, if not disgusted, with the way those companies operated—the *mis*management, *miss*ed opportunities, *mis*treatment.

So many misses!

The more they think about it, the more they yearn for the chance to have a hit, to build an organization on their values, one that will maximize profit and its people's potential. Their organizations will be innovative, react nimbly to markets, and grow at a steady clip. They will surround themselves with talented, hardworking people and create the place where they always wanted to work.

For a while, sometimes many years, the dream inches toward reality. Founders surround themselves with hardworking people who believe in the same thing, communicate well, and work together on targets. Profits start to flow, and the business grows. "Business" actually feels like the wrong word for what they're creating. This thing that began as a dream is alive and growing. This thing has a soul.

The team expands, and before long, founders are no longer pleased with everyone, but maybe this is inevitable, just as growth was bound to make communicating tougher. It's hard to say exactly where or why communication is failing these days, but too many fires need dousing now to worry about that.

Profits aren't quite where the owners hoped. They implement a business operating system, or they introduce various business-school measures (there's now an MBA, or several, in the picture). Improvement comes in fits and starts, but they keep bumping into that invisible something that drains the momentum, and they can't seem to break through. Key projects stall and important tasks slip. Too many employees lack drive and initiative. The status quo is seeping in. Owners have never worked harder or had less to show for their effort. They have never needed a vacation more or felt less able to take one. Their stomachs churn at the thought that the horrible old cliché has come true—they aren't running the business, it's running them.

What happened to the dream? It has become something awful—a company or, worse yet, a business. The once-living thing has morphed into a soulless machine. Like a machine, it is static and rigid. It can't grow, evolve, or adapt, and founders aren't sure where things went wrong.

This is when we meet most of the people we work with—some desperate, others only dissatisfied, but all aware of a significant gap between their original vision and the dysfunction they now see on a daily basis. The root of the problem—and the argument at the heart of this book—is that they are not running courageously patient organizations with BITE. In this section we will explain exactly what we mean by a courageously patient organization and introduce the Seven Promises based on the Seven Critical Needs that can transform even the most dysfunctional business into one with high levels of measurable BITE.

Courage and patience are much more than virtues. Instilled in an organization through the Seven Promises, they motivate team members who belong, who believe, who are accountable to make decisions that align with your objectives to realize a vision that makes you a fierce competitor. Courage and patience actively repel, empowering your leaders, managers, and you to have hard conversations with team members who don't belong or believe so that they self-select out to find a better fit elsewhere. The courage and patience to repel people before they join strengthens your organizational health, improves your organizational culture, and makes life less stressful for everyone who might have to work with those who do not buy in, repelling them before they have a chance to destroy your BITE.

In case the notion of Seven Promises implies otherwise, we want to point out right away that this is not an easy process. Just like Patrick Lencioni, author of *The Five Dysfunctions of a Team*, says about a company taking on a core values initiative, an organization considering the journey to become a courageously patient organization with BITE must first come to grips with the fact that when properly done, it will inflict pain. The Seven Promises will hold leaders to a higher standard and make some of your teammates feel like outcasts. Teammates will hold each other accountable. Difficult conversations—the type that so many of us avoid like the plague— will be had. Getting back to your dream will not necessarily be a walk in the park. Some pain is unavoidable, and the act of making a promise will give you courage.

Very few moral judgments are more intuitively obvious and widely shared than this: ***Promises are made to be kept.*** Making and keeping promises takes courage and patience; for most of us they are not entered into lightly. This is the power we are trying to harness.

A feature of promises that make them interesting to us as we build an intentional culture is their role in producing trust, trust that facilitates social coordination and cooperation.

As business owners, we don't think much about the connection between promises and our organizational health. We understand contractual and commercial promises, but we often overlook the advantages we could harness if we applied the same amount of rigor to our cultural promises.

Unlike everyday moral duties, the duty to not steal, for example, promises are not owed equally to everyone, but rather, only to those to whom we have made a promise. Further, promises are voluntary; we don't have to make promises, but we must keep them when we do.

Promises are created *by* acts of will. When I promise to do something, it means that, by doing so, I have created the obligation to do it.

The idea that we simply manufacture promissory obligations by speaking them, like an incantation, is a decidedly mysterious and powerful feature of promises. As Scottish philosopher David Hume remarked in *A Treatise of Human Nature* (1739–40):*

> I shall further observe, that, since every new promise imposes a new obligation of morality on the person who promises, and since this new obligation arises from his will; it is one of the most mysterious and incomprehensible operations that can possibly be imagined, and may even be compared to *transubstantiation* or *holy orders*, where a certain form of words,

---

* Emphasis in the original.

along with a certain intention, changes entirely the nature of an external object, and even of a human creature.

Patience, as we'll explore shortly, has nothing to do with dragging feet, suffering fools, or reacting sluggishly. A courageously patient organization takes the time to focus, rising above the system to make methodical improvements, and to prioritize problems and opportunities. Patience and courage lead to consistency and stamina, and they attract employees who love their work and repel those who don't. When team members, and the business as a whole, enjoy positive alignment on the Seven Critical Needs, they create a courageously patient organization that runs smoothly and gains a massive edge over the competition.

## BITE, Courage, and Patience Are Industry Agnostic

Our concept of BITE and a courageously patient organization anchored in the Seven Critical Needs is the distillation of 35 years' experience. Issues and goals vary widely from owner to owner and business to business, but when someone asks what sorts of organizations the seven can help, I pretend to think deeply, then smile and say unironically: "the kind with people."

> *When someone asks what sorts of organizations the seven can help, I pretend to think deeply, then smile and say unironically: "the kind with people."*

In one recent week, we spent Monday with the leaders of the Wake County (North Carolina) SPCA, which has 78 people on payroll and hundreds of volunteers; Tuesday at an industrial rigging company that employs 1,180 people; Wednesday with an 18-person commercial real estate firm; Thursday with the team overseeing 781 people at the Oak Ridge Laboratory in Tennessee; and Friday with a team that runs 14 swim schools that employ 148 people. The next week we worked with the senior leadership team of Sandia National Labs, which has 23,469 employees. All these organizations are benefiting enormously from embracing the Seven Critical Needs as we help them create measurable BITE Scores on their way to becoming courageously patient organizations.

As we often tell leaders, the language of a courageously patient organization is industry agnostic. Small or enormous, for profit or nonprofit, heavy manufacturing, software, or customer service—if the operation has people, running it well requires courage and patience. Throughout the book we will give concrete examples to show in practical terms how *positively aligning with* the seven can help all owners and leaders create courageously patient organizations that drive with their vision.

## All Problems Are People Problems

Every problem in an organization is, at its root, a people problem. Corporations exist on paper, but they aren't real entities without the people who comprise them. As my father, Walter Jr., a dedicated retailer running 14 stores with 2,100 employees, used to say, "It would be easy if it weren't for the people."

As coaches who help senior leadership teams as part of our EOS Implementation Practices, no one knows this better than we do. We typically work with 25 or so teams at a time, meeting with each for five full days a year. This means that more than one-third of our days, around 135 per year, are spent in rooms with senior leadership. Most of the issues and problems we uncover during sessions ultimately have to do with people.

The frustration with people is understandable. Around 70 percent of US workers are not actively engaged at work, according to a recent Gallup survey. Business owners often cite Gallup's famous engagement stats—some have them memorized—and all can supply anecdotal evidence of problems with team members and a work ethic that seems to have slipped.

Every three years Gallup does a US employee engagement survey, and the numbers typically look like this: 15/49/36. Think of the dashed line in the illustration as representing "neutral" energy/engagement. Above the dashed line people are putting energy into your organization; below, they are taking it out.

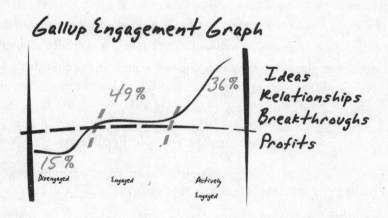

Nearly one-third of folks, 36 percent, are engaged or actively engaged at work. This is where the magic happens, where the new ideas are formed, where the profitable and creative relationships are established.

Half of the folks, 49 percent, are just "energy-neutral engaged." There are a couple of awareness points we like to make with our clients around this 49 percent. One is that we must have these folks. They are the boxcars in the freight train, happily carrying heavy loads, staying in line. They don't drag their brakes, but they don't add a lot of energy like the engaged "engines" do either. We have them and need them, and you need to embrace that they are just fine as neutrally engaged and work to keep them happy.

The last group makes up 15 percent of workers, and they are disengaged or actively disengaged, robbing energy. We ask when coaching if anyone knows who we are talking about, can they picture one of these faces, and almost 100 percent of the time folks give a resounding yes. We also ask how many engaged team members it takes to offset a disengaged employee. Gallup says the ratio is 1:1; our clients say 3:1. One client, Michael, put it this way: "Let's have a race. I am going to run around messing up the house, and you go around, cleaning the house. Who is going to win?" It's an effective way of illustrating how one actively disengaged employee can offset multiple engaged employees, and it always gets a chuckle.

Discovery 1: I was trained in and fell in love with Gallup's Q12 approach to employee engagement in 2006, before I started implementing EOS, and in my early implementation years I tried hard to make the Q12 line up to and make sense with the tools of EOS—there just was not a clear bridge that could be easily crossed. The seven are deeper, more actionable derivatives of the Q12.

## The Q12—The 12 Questions Gallup Uses to Measure Employee Engagement

1. Do you know what is expected of you at work?
2. Do you have the materials and equipment to do your work right?

3. At work, do you have the opportunity to do what you do best every day?

4. In the last seven days, have you received recognition or praise for doing good work?

5. Does your supervisor, or someone at work, seem to care about you as a person?

6. Is there someone at work who encourages your development?

7. At work, do your opinions seem to count?

8. Does the mission/purpose of your company make you feel your job is important?

9. Are your associates (fellow employees) committed to doing quality work?

10. Do you have a best friend at work?

11. In the last six months, has someone at work talked to you about your progress?

12. In the last year, have you had opportunities to learn and grow?

I am a believer in the Q12 and the power of employee engagement, yet . . .

Discovery 2: The way Gallup was grouping people was not what my clients and I were seeing in the real world. Most of my clients came in with okay organizational health and they generally had a bunch of positive-energy people. There was always a lesser amount of neutral people, and there were negative people. Once my clients started using the BITE7 Survey and BITE Index, the pattern that emerged was similar to Gallup in one way: the group BITE labeled negative was about the same percent that Gallup labeled disengaged. We saw, confirmed, and now believe most people don't live in neutral, they go to the ends as seen diagrammed in our BITE Index Graph.

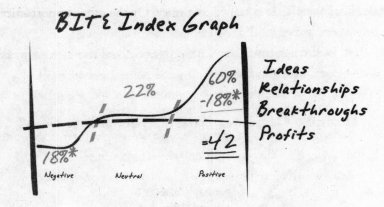

*BITE Index Graph*

22%

60%
-18%*

Ideas
Relationships
Breakthroughs
Profits

=42

18%*

Negative    Neutral    Positive

Why is someone negative/disengaged? *Because they care.* Team members become negative/disengaged because they care deeply about something that *you* are not providing. Often, you can turn a negative/actively disengaged team member into a positive/actively engaged team member by finding out what that thing is. The answer is in the Seven Critical Needs.

I like to describe this phenomenon using the graphic "Danger/Opportunity Gap," or sometimes I call it the "I Care Gap." I draw the BITE curve as a circle, with the two ends at the top forming the gap. When we pull the two ends together at the top of the accompanying Danger/Opportunity Gap graph, we see that the distance between positive and negative is very small, and it is easier to lose someone to the dark side/negativity/disengagement than it is to move a neutral employee to active positive engagement. Why? Because the people at the top care. Think about yourself as a positive, engaged employee. Will you be happy living in neutral BITE? No! If something goes sideways that you care about, you can become negative, disruptive, playing out the same dysfunction that is brought by an actively disengaged person. That is the danger.

The opposite is also true. Very often we have a negative, disengaged person who just needs to get to positive alignment, and we can move them over. That is our opportunity. Or the other opportunity is to help them understand they are miserable, not bought in, don't feel included, lack trust, and are just disengaged, and we can help them self-select out, which is illustrated by the pigtail arrow: repel.

## "Danger/Opportunity Gap" or "I Care Gap"

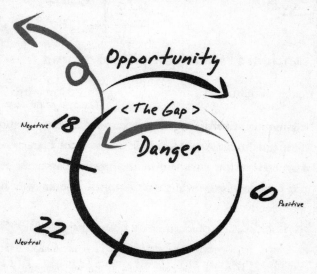

Don't waste all your best efforts trying to move neutral folks to positive. Work hard to keep your positive folks positive and to make the negative folks become positive—or get them to self-select out of your organization. Remember: courageously patient organizations have the power and clarity to attract—pull them over like a magnet—or repel them.

Key point: In the future, after you have adopted the BITE7 approach, your Seven Promises will act as a repellant during your interview process. You will be sharing your Seven Promises with potential teammates, describing in detail what it means to be positively aligned. You will say something like, "If you can align to these seven things, it will be like nirvana, you will love it here; if you can't, it will feel like hell on earth. This organization does not tolerate people who do not help keep the promises, and you will be drummed out, fair enough?" You will be shooing bad fits away before they join so you do not have to go through the act of weeding them out. Your positive people will thank you for it and reward you by hanging around.

## Lencioni's "Healthy and Smart" and Trust

Patrick Lencioni defines "healthy" as an organization with:

- Little to no confusion
- that leads to little to no politics
- that leads to low turnover in *key* people*
- and high levels of productivity and engagement.

(*Note: A player, our key people, hate confusion and especially politics.)

We measure engagement with the Seven Question BITE Survey and the BITE Index; we measure productivity in other ways.

Lencioni's pyramid model for teamwork is another model our clients love. Lencioni argues that without high levels of vulnerability-based trust, or psychological safety, according to Harvard Business School professor Amy Edmondson and Google's Project Aristotle, which I present later in chapter 2, you will not enjoy healthy, open, and honest conflict and debate. Without honest, healthy conflict and debate, you will not get commitment, only compliance, and without commitment, the team will hesitate in calling a teammate out on not fulfilling their commitment—a "WTF" moment, and we don't mean "Wow, That's Fantastic." Without the ability to drive accountability in their teammates, overall results are going to suffer.

## Lencioni's Pyramid Model

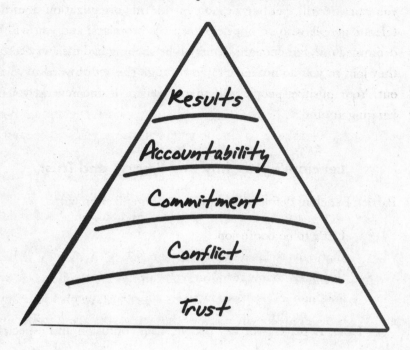

You can measure your levels of organizational trust by using the Seven Question BITE Survey and the BITE Index. High BITE scores reflect higher levels of trust and psychological safety, which lead to more robust debate.

Yet there are some people you just cannot work with, and the Seven Critical Needs and their subsequent Seven Promises will not fix them. Courageous leaders counsel these people out of the organization with firmness, respect, and class.

## A Focus on Millennials and Gen Z Teammates

Millennials, the generation starting in 1981, account for 38 percent of the US workforce, rising to an estimated 75 percent of US workers by

2025. Their younger Gen Z counterparts were born starting in 1997. The future health of our economy depends on harnessing the energy of all these workers.

Only 29 percent of millennials were engaged at work in 2022, according to Gallup's study, "How Millennials Want to Work and Live," and a record 60 percent of them are open to new job opportunities—a higher percentage than previous generations. But when you look at the macro stats about engagement, you see the numbers are basically the same: 32/50/18.

That gap between perception and reality is the foundation for this book and the start of a 10-year journey for us, doing grounded theory and soft-skills research, observing patterns, and building on decades of our own experience in business.

As I mentioned in the introduction, the spark that led to *Attract or Repel* was simply that the millennials and Gen Z colleagues we met were capable, talented team players eager to take on leadership roles. We could not reconcile many of the stereotypes about millennials, for instance, with our experience of team members, like Kerrie, a 28-year-old company president, doing an exemplary job of integrating an $8 million-per-year business with 67 employees.

What inspired Kerrie and the other hardworking millennials we met, and what made them actively engaged? They desire the same things we all do. They want to feel a strong sense of belonging at work: a belief in the core values of their company and the confidence that they have the skills needed to do their jobs. The ones we spoke to wanted to be held accountable, and a lack of clear accountability left them frustrated. They wanted to feel like they were serving a larger purpose—don't we all?—but many of their leaders seemed unable to articulate their organization's *why*, or merely paid it lip service. The millennials we speak to now long to feel confident in the ways they were measured and heard and developed. Leaders who provided that confidence through clear channels received a high level of engagement, trust, and performance in return. Those who did not blamed the confusion and frustration they sowed—often with the best of intentions—on the supposedly poor motivation of a generation.

We quickly came to realize that what we were learning about millennials applied to all team members, whether 18 years old or 80. They answered our questions about satisfaction and frustrations at work in many ways, some at length and some briefly, some with great precision, and others with vague unease. Some couldn't wait to go to work in the morning, and some dreaded walking into the office, but the same patterns kept emerging.

After years of these discussions, we noticed that the important issues mirrored the same ones I'd encountered running my own four companies. I'd addressed them in various ways as a business owner but never spelled them out as I was starting to in my work with leadership teams. As coaches, we eventually were able to distill those years of feedback into the seven fundamentals at the heart of this book—the Seven Critical Needs that form the backbone of the Seven Promises. The Seven Promises must be kept to nurture high levels of measurable BITE—buy-in, inclusion, trust, and engagement.

| Seven Critical Needs Statements | | |
|---|---|---|
| **The Seven Needs** | **For the Individual** | **For the Organization** |
| **To Belong** | I understand and embrace our organization's core values, and I have (or can develop) the skills my job and roles require. **I belong.** | We have clearly defined our core values and have mechanisms in place to hire, reward, adjust, and terminate around them, and we have defined all skills necessary for every job and role. |
| **To Believe** | I know and believe in my organization's *why.* I also believe in our leadership, my teammates, our strategic direction, and the products and services we provide. **I believe.** | We know our *why,* our focus, and our strategic direction. We have mechanisms in place to clearly and consistently communicate our strategies for achieving it. |
| **To Be Accountable** | I understand and embrace the purpose of my job and roles that make up my job. I know what I should be thinking about and doing and why. **I am accountable.** | Our accountability and responsibility structure is clear; it is captured, communicated, and consistently updated. |
| **To Be Measured** | I understand and embrace how and why I am measured, and I know what constitutes a good job. My measures give me direction and help me to form strategies to do great work in all of my roles. **I am measured.** | We have SMART— specific, measurable, attainable, reviewable, time-bound—metrics for our jobs and roles. Team members use them to form strategies for success. |

| Seven Critical Needs Statements | | |
|---|---|---|
| **The Seven Needs** | **For the Individual** | **For the Organization** |
| **To Be Heard** | I understand and embrace how and when my organization listens and responds. **I am heard.** | We have clear, consistent communication mechanisms and channels in place. They promote listening and responding, help build trust, spur debate, solve problems, and allow individuals to participate in being heard. |
| **To Be Developed** | I understand and embrace my organization's development mechanisms and how I can develop; I know how to take an active role in my own development. **I am developed.** | We have consistent, repeatable mechanisms in place that help team members take charge of their own development. |
| **To Be Balanced** | I understand and embrace my organization's definition of balance and the mechanisms I can participate in to reach my goal of balance. **I am balanced.** | Our organization's definition of balance is clear and consistently communicated. We have work-life, compensation, and health and wellness mechanisms in place for people to participate in maintaining their own balance. |

These seven principles, we discovered, were the things that made not just millennials, but all employees, feel enabled and engaged, that made them love going to work. The Seven Critical Needs were simple.

Getting team members and the organizations to positively align on all of them was not, but once we understood we had a key that could unlock success for any organization willing to use it, my team and I knew we had to write this book. (The entire framework in this book has been a discovery—a discovery revealed by working with my client teams and their millennials. We discovered the list and almost everything else together. So, throughout this book, I'll often say "we" to refer to this team. We created it together; I only listened, put it together, tested it through trial and error.)

Excited about the Seven Critical Needs, we drilled down further and realized that courage and patience built on BITE make up the foundation they rest on. Courage and patience had been on our mind. In our conversations with millennials, we came to understand that if they differed at all from previous generations, it was perhaps because they had more clarity about what they wanted and a little more wisdom when it came to their futures. That wisdom gave them the courage to not simply accept the status quo or some prescribed route, or to take what someone handed them without the ability to change their circumstances. They were courageous about shaping the right futures for themselves, and they thrived as members of courageously patient organizations.

# CHAPTER 2

# Courage and Patience Built on BITE

**DIGGING DEEPER, MY** team and I discovered that the common thread tying these Seven Critical Needs together was courage and patience. Positive alignment to the Seven Critical Needs created high levels of measurable BITE and built perseverance, wisdom, and grit into organizations. It helped them to establish an authentic vision and create the goals and strategies to realize it. It created an approach that is best described as courageously patient. Positively aligning to the Seven Critical Needs makes your company a courageously patient organization with BITE.

Courage is choosing the hard right over the easy wrong. In organizations, courage is having a difficult conversation when it would be easier and less awkward to avoid it. Courage is honoring your promise when it would be easier to break it. Courage is taking the blame and admitting your mistakes when it would be easier to deflect it onto someone or something else. Courage is overcoming the discomfort of vulnerability to allow others to see you for who you really are when it would be easier to pretend to be someone you're not. Most importantly, courage is having the *patience* to make decisions that honor your core values and mission in a time of crisis when it would be easier to react out of fear. Dysfunctional organizations are hostile to employees who make courageous decisions. Courageous organizations, on the other hand, reward courage and make it contagious.

We are arguing that courage and patience are built on buy-in, inclusion, trust, and engagement: BITE. They are the measurable key results of aligning on each of the Seven Critical Needs, and BITE drives our ultimate measurable output: significantly improved financial performance.

## Employee Engagement

In "The Benefits of Employee Engagement," Gallup's statistics argue that when you move your organization to the top employee engagement quartile, you will enjoy these types of results:

- 10 percent better customer loyalty
- 20 percent better sales results
- 24 percent less turnover in high-turnover orgs
- 59 percent less turnover in low-turnover orgs
- 40 percent fewer errors and quality defects
- 70 percent fewer safety incidents
- 41 percent less absenteeism
- 21 percent bottom-line improvements

You can do your own math to understand if any of these changes will manifest as profit in your organization. The BITE7 Framework drives measurable employee engagement, and the results we see are similar to the Gallup numbers.

When it comes to workplace trust, a frequently referenced study by Andy Atkins with Interaction Associates, Inc., "Building Workplace Trust: Trends and High Performance," gives us some numbers.

Atkins's study compares high-trust organizations (trust leaders) to low-trust organizations (non-leaders) by measuring employee opinions:

He asks, "How effective is your organization at achieving 'x' business outcome?" He captured the percentage of the employees who answered "extremely" and "very likely."

| Question | Trust Leaders | Trust Non-leaders |
|---|---|---|
| Customer loyalty and retention | 84% | 54% |
| Competitive market position | 76% | 48% |
| Predictable business and financial results | 74% | 38% |
| Profit growth | 65% | 39% |
| **Average** | 75% | 45% |

Another finding from Atkins's study is that "high-trust companies (trust leaders) are more than 2½ times more likely to be high-performing revenue organizations than low-trust companies."

The numbers from Gallup and Atkins correlate closely with the results our client organizations are experiencing. When companies embrace the BITE7 Framework and use it to strengthen the effectiveness of their business operating system, they enjoy measurable improvements in their buy-in, inclusion, trust, and engagement scores, which translate directly into financial results.

One clear example is demonstrated with a case study we call "Two Apples."

## Two Apples Case Study

Same business, same industry, same size, same vendors, same enterprise resource planning software (ERP), same sales coach, same EOS Implementer, same buying group, same web solutions, same southern markets, both over 50 years old.

Company A (Co A) is a year into their EOS journey with Uncle Walt and the seven. They are still working on rolling it all the way out as organizational promises.

Company B (Co B) is three years in and has fully rolled EOS out on top of the seven, using the complete system. The Seven Promises have been made and are being kept. Co B is a courageously patient organization with BITE.

Three years ago, Co B had a 59 BITE and was delivering to industry averages. As you can see in the chart, it is exceeding industry averages, and Co A is well on its way.

| Measure | Industry | Co A | Co B |
|---|---|---|---|
| EBITDA | 1.2% | 2.1% | 7.6% |
| Gross margin % | 29.5 | 30.2 | 32.6 |
| Gross margin $s/FTE | $100,000 | $125,789 | $146,356 |
| Day's sales receivables | 40 days | 33 days | 29 days |
| Fill rate | 93% | 94% | 98% |
| BITE Index | 59 | 63 | 87 |

I will let my accounting nerd background combine with my love of BITE to dig a little deeper.

EBITDA—earnings before interest, taxes, depreciation, and amortization—is a working capital measurement. These mature distribution companies live in a very price-competitive world. Remember the Gallup numbers, 20 percent better sales results, 10 percent better customer loyalty? Co B with the 87 BITE has employees who are bought in and believe. This is driving the gross margin dollars/full-time equivalent—customers are buying more and paying more, orders are larger, economies of scale are kicking in all because Co B employees are positively aligned to the seven; they are courageously leaning into their customer relationships with confidence, and this confidence is contagious.

We have been working with Co B for a while now, and in one year, the company had a few key people out for various reasons, and those absences dragged their president/integrator down into the weeds. According to her people, she lost sight of the promises, the company's BITE Index slipped, and their financial results slipped too; it is a yin and yang deal.

Moral: the Seven Promises, coupled to an effective BOS, directed by your BITE scores, will drive financial performance.

## Courage

We have introduced the idea of a courageously patient organization as a model for businesses, but we need to look more closely at courage. Dictionary definitions refer to an ability to endure difficulties and to maintain calm when faced with problems. Nelson Mandela observed that "courage is not the absence of fear, but the triumph over it. The brave man is not he who does not feel afraid, but he who conquers that fear." John Wayne shared a similar understanding: "Courage is being scared to death . . . and saddling up anyway." The Cadet Prayer at West Point stresses the importance of courage when it implores cadets to "choose the harder right instead of the easier wrong." These are all outstanding definitions of courage, and our meaning of courage includes all these things. However, courage in an organization is unique, and our thinking on organizational courage and courageous leaders has been shaped in profound ways by the work of Patrick Lencioni and Brené Brown.

In *The Five Dysfunctions of a Team*, Lencioni explains that courage is essential to having tough conversations and holding people accountable. Success, he asserts, "all comes down to real people having the courage to sit down with one another and accept the discomfort that is necessary to improve." Continuous improvement cannot be sustained without courageous conversations because only by having everyone share ideas and argue for which is best will a company make the best decisions. And good decisions are useless if members of an organization don't have the courage to hold each other accountable to them.

Similarly, Brené Brown, in *Dare to Lead*, shares that in researching business culture, the number one problem businesses have, as reported by business leaders, is "avoiding tough conversations, including giving honest, productive feedback. Some leaders attributed this to a lack of courage . . . Whatever the reason, there was a saturation across the data that the consequence is a lack of clarity, diminishing trust and engagement, and an increase in problematic behavior." According to Brown, the solution to avoidance is for daring leaders to "choose courage over comfort; choose what's right over what's fun, fast, or easy; and practice their values, not just profess them."

So, when we use the word "courage" when discussing PBOLTs and their leadership teams, we mean choosing the hard right over the easy wrong: choosing to have a hard conversation with a colleague who isn't behaving up to the standards he or she agreed to; to take the blame when it would be easier to deflect it onto someone, or something, else; or to honor the Seven Promises you made to the organization when it would be easier to forget about them. Courageous leaders are committed to building BITE into their organization, and they choose to work though the discomfort necessary to do so.

## Psychological Safety: Google's Project Aristotle

Another researched and statistically valid concept, which comes out of Harvard's Amy Edmondson and Google's Project Aristotle, is that of psychological safety and its effectiveness on teams. In Google's multi-year study around what makes great teams, the number one driver was psychological safety where "team members feel safe to take risks and be vulnerable in front of each other."

In 2012, Google embarked on a quest to figure out what made their company's teams effective. They called the study "Project Aristotle" to honor the ancient Greek philosopher's observation that in some groups—and on some teams—the whole is greater than the sum of its parts. They chose 180 Google teams and measured everything they could think of. Then they set about figuring out why successful teams soared while other teams couldn't get off the ground.

After collecting all the data and researching all the academic theories on team success, they were stuck. They couldn't find any common threads between successful teams in terms of gender, personality type, friendships outside of work, motivations, or backgrounds.

They got unstuck, and fast, when they came across research by Harvard Business School professor Amy Edmondson on "psychological safety," which she defined as a "shared belief held by members of a team that the team is safe for interpersonal risk-taking . . . a sense of confidence that the team will not embarrass, reject, or punish someone for speaking up . . . It describes a team climate characterized by interpersonal trust and mutual respect in which people are comfortable being themselves."

While there isn't a single formula for creating psychological safety, there are some best practices to keep in mind. In 2008, a group of professors from Carnegie Mellon, MIT, and Union College tried to study the intelligence of groups. One of their discoveries was that when it came to group performance, the sum of individual IQs mattered far less than how teammates treated one another. They argue the right norms could raise a group's collective intelligence, whereas the wrong norms could hobble a team, even if, individually, all the members were exceptionally bright.

One of those best practices is that groups should discuss the norms they want to guide group behavior before getting started on a project. And the researchers in the 2008 study found two norms that every team should consider: First, on the good teams in the study, members spoke in roughly the same proportion. In a *New York Times* article by Charles Duhigg, researcher Anita Wooley explained, "as long as everyone got a chance to talk, the team did well, but if only one person or a small group spoke all the time, the collective intelligence declined." Second, the good teams all had high "average social sensitivity"—a fancy way of saying they were skilled at intuiting how others felt based on their tone of voice, their expressions, and other nonverbal cues. They were better than bad teams at paying attention to each other's feelings.

In other words, both studies found that who was on the team was less important than how the team worked together. Good teams create trust, belonging, and inclusion. The norms they establish ensure fairness and respect. Everyone is invited to contribute. Everyone is more concerned with "getting it right" than "being right." And finally, teammates care about each other as human beings. These norms create an environment where team members feel safe to take risks, which in turn allows the group to reach its full potential.

Before we move on, you may be curious about other norms Google researchers found to be important for group success. While psychological safety was far and away the most important, there were four others, and you should be able to see a lot of overlap with our Seven Critical Needs:

**Dependability**: On dependable teams, members reliably complete quality work on time (vs. the opposite—shirking responsibilities).

**Structure and clarity**: An individual's understanding of job expectations, the process for fulfilling these expectations, and the consequences of one's performance are important for team effectiveness. Goals can be set at the individual or group level and must be specific, challenging, and attainable. Google often uses objectives and key results (OKRs) to help set and communicate short- and long-term goals.

**Meaning**: Finding a sense of purpose in either the work itself or the output is important for team effectiveness. The meaning of work is personal and can vary: financial security, supporting family, helping the team succeed, or self-expression for each individual, for example.

**Impact**: The results of one's work—the subjective judgment that your work is making a difference—is important for teams. Seeing that one's work is contributing to the organization's goals can help reveal impact.

So, how can you increase psychological safety on your own team? Find the answers to your Seven Questions and turn them into Seven Promises.

The BITE Framework, coupled with an effective BOS, will establish the right norms and build psychological safety.

This matrix shows how the Seven Critical Needs and Promises ensure that the Google researchers' top five norms/ingredients for high-performing teams are supported and systematized. We are arguing that positive alignment with the Seven Critical Needs creates psychological safety. Alignment around these critical needs drives dependability, structure, and clarity and is supported when people believe and belong because they have needed skills, they are accountable, own their measures, participate in being heard, and learn where they need to leave the drama at home. Meaning and impact are supported when what they are asked to believe in is clear. Impact is made through clear delivery of skills; individuals will embrace accountability, measurement, communication, constant learning, and a balanced work environment. When we get clear on what alignment means to the Seven Critical Needs, we support all of Project Aristotle's findings.

| | Belong | Believe | Accountable | Measured | Heard | Developed | Balanced |
|---|---|---|---|---|---|---|---|
| Psychological Safety | ✓ | ✓ | ✓ | ✓ | ✓ | ✓ | ✓ |
| Dependability | ✓ | ✓ | ✓ | ✓ | ✓ | ✓ | ✓ |
| Structure and Clarity | ✓ | ✓ | ✓ | ✓ | ✓ | ✓ | ✓ |
| Meaning | ✓ | ✓ | ✓ | ✓ | ✓ | ✓ | ✓ |
| Impact | ✓ | ✓ | ✓ | ✓ | ✓ | ✓ | ✓ |

Finally, we'd like to share one more take on courage, this one from the famous British writer and theologian C. S. Lewis in *The Screwtape Letters*: "Courage is not simply one of the virtues, but the form of every virtue at the testing point." A leader may create an organization founded upon the most wonderful values and virtues imaginable, but without courage, those values and virtues will collapse in the face of great difficulty. Courage must be built and reinforced in every aspect of an organization for it to thrive during times of crisis, and maintaining positive alignment to the Seven Critical Needs helps a leader do just that. Keep this in mind later when we discuss the first critical need: *to belong* and core values. Core values are essential to robust organizational health and success, but they are impotent without courage.

What do we mean by "core values"? The phrase has become popular in business circles, but even many of those promoting the idea seem unsure of its meaning. We define core values as the philosophy or attitude that shapes how team members treat each other, clients, and other stakeholders. Core values are the deeply held principles that set the organization apart, giving it its unique personality and a competitive edge. They are the cultural foundation beneath every meeting, memo, and watercooler conversation.

At the sailing gear dot-com, Layline, our core values could be summarized as PC3: be positive, cheerful, cognizant, challenge your work, and try to ask three questions before you answer one. These were the key elements of a mindset that we wanted to inform every decision and color every interaction—whether with a coworker, a customer, a vendor, or me. A large software and client-service company we have worked with describes its core values as: passionate, disciplined, client focused, dependable, and engaged. Another client, a grocery store chain, lists its core values as: take ownership, treat customers like family, work well with teammates, and be willing to learn and improve.

These organizations have very different core values. Each set reflects the personality of the organization, its vision, and the attitude of team members. Being *client focused* and *dependable* has a different nuance than *treating customers like family*. Neither approach is better than the other. Each reflects a unique mindset at the heart of how a particular organization does business. A team member who excels at being client focused and dependable might recoil at the idea of treating customers like family or always asking three questions before answering one. Such a person might align with the core values of the software company in my example but struggle for years without ever aligning to positive alignment at Layline or the grocery chain.

We are providing examples here to illustrate what true core values are and how they work on a practical level. When we do this in conversations with leaders and business owners, they frequently realize that the things posted on the company website, hung above the reception desk, or printed in the training manual do not represent the organization's true core values.

We have also found that it's helpful and sometimes even more illuminating to consider what core values are *not*.

**A core value is not a goal.** Endless companies now list some version of "a sustainable future" as a core value. Sorry, that's a goal, not a value. It does not describe the way team members interact with each other and customers on a daily basis. Patrick Lencioni, who wrote *The Five Dysfunctions of a Team* and many other books and articles on the subject, has shaped my thinking on core values as much as anyone. He makes the point that an aspiration is not a core value and recounts the story of a Fortune 500 CEO telling him without hesitation that "a sense of urgency" is a core value at his organization because *no one has it yet*. Aspirations are important—*we need to become more X or have more Y*—but should not be confused with core values. Core values represent today's deeply held attitude, not tomorrow's target.

**A core value is not an obvious baseline.** Qualities like honesty, integrity, and trustworthiness sound like core values, but short of organized crime syndicates, every team member at every organization should have these qualities, right? Lencioni calls such attributes "permission-to-play" values. They represent a minimum behavioral standard throughout society and don't distinguish an organization in any way. They are not core values.

**A core value is not marketing.** Once upon a time, a large company I've heard of trademarked the phrase "culture of caring" and insisted in its marketing that in addition to being "warm, welcoming and humble," its team members would be empathetic enough to make a difference in people's lives. In 2016, news emerged that, to collect bonuses, thousands of the employees were opening fraudulent accounts customers hadn't authorized. The warm, fuzzy lines on the website suddenly looked like empty slogans. Core values are internal and sacrosanct, as Lencioni says. They are the secret sauce that creates courage and momentum for a company. If it makes sense to use them in some marketing materials, fine, but first and foremost, they must be the internal engine running the organization. Hollow announcements of generic core values have a way of coming back to bite you on the rear end.

**A core value is not a skill or an IQ.** Most business owners want smart employees, but most also know that intelligence doesn't automatically mean "team player." If we hired a genius at Layline who thought he had all the answers and didn't need to ask questions, he wouldn't last long. If a medical practice establishes "personal warmth" and "a friendly bedside manner" as a core value, plenty of skilled but socially awkward surgeons won't belong there.

**A core value is not cookie cutter or industry specific.** Core values come from deep soul searching about what's important to and special about an organization. When they're real, they attract and inspire people who belong. When platitudes are fired off instead, they create cynicism, not inspiration, attracting people who simply need jobs. One client of mine frames the company's core values this way: "We believe in the power of listening, hearing and taking action." There's no way for you to guess that this is a janitorial supply firm, but seeing the way the organization integrates those deeply held values into its operation, we can tell you, is inspiring. This is what's important to the company's leaders and separates it from the competition.

**A core value is not accidental.** As the center of the dream that becomes a business, core values often gestate for years within the business owner before they guide his or her company. Over time, additional values often gestate within the organization—Lencioni calls them "accidental values." They might be positive or negative, but they are unintentional. They should be watched closely and not confused with core values.

**A core value is not a political candidate.** Which is to say, the process of deciding on your core values is not a democratic one. It falls on the leadership team and owner—not on all employees. Remember the start of this section, where we said that around 80 percent of determining positive alignment to the critical need *to belong* falls on the organization. Owners had certain principles in mind when they began turning their dream into the reality of a business. There are particular attitudes that they would like to hear in the hallways, see conveyed in reports, and have transmitted to clients. Passing the responsibility for articulating those core values to employees is disingenuous and likely to result in chaos.

How should core values be articulated? By way of background, we highly recommend Patrick Lencioni's *Harvard Business Review* article "Make Your Values Mean Something."

## Patience

We all know that patience is a virtue, but I doubt very many business owners consider it to be a particularly sexy business trait. But I'm quite certain the PBOLTs who read this book will feel differently about the value of patience when they see how patience gives a company a competitive edge.

Explaining what we *don't* mean by patience is perhaps the best starting point.

**Patience does not mean slowness.** It often requires slowing down to focus, reflect, and prioritize, but a patient organization has a methodology that actually allows for smart responses to be made quickly. Patience has nothing to do with foot-dragging, procrastination, or putting off important decisions. Patience means having a system and a set of decision matrices in place to make it easier to strike when the time is right, at lightning speed if necessary.

**Patience does not mean putting up with organizational terrorists or poor fits.** No business owner starts out dreaming of surrounding himself with jerks, but they have a way of creeping into organizations over time. Jerks force leaders to spend hours keeping people happy. Jerks rob organizations of time, energy, and courage. Ultimately, they manifest as what I refer to as "organizational terrorists," holding teammates hostage and destroying the culture owners once dreamed of. Terrorists do not share the business's core values and must go. Tolerating poor fits is charity and insanity, not patience. Remember: attract or repel.

**Patience does not mean avoidance.** Patience, like courage, does not look for ways to go around things; it goes through them. Again, having a patient system in place allows leaders to make the tough calls rather than avoiding them, to trek down a difficult path rather than take a shortcut to avoid pain.

**Patience is not passivity.** Patience is extremely active. It is about doing, but the doing is always accompanied by thinking. Often, it is downright aggressive as it confronts a problem or seizes an opportunity. Indecision is at the opposite end of the spectrum from patience. Inaction within a system is not patience. Patience comes from rising above the system to actively improve it.

## What Is Courageous Patience in Business?

Steve Jobs might be the poster boy. He was one of the most courageous and patient leaders we can think of—and one of the most active. He was thoughtful, figured out what he wanted and how to get there, and then attacked it with grit. Everyone knows his visionary role in bringing the personal computer to the mass market, but they forget that he also traveled through India, studying Zen Buddhism in search of enlightenment just before co-founding Apple. They remember his revival of the company in the '90s and the cultural revolution he wrought but forget that he spent a decade at the mostly unprofitable NeXT, Inc., trying and failing and trying again as he developed the vision that would ultimately lead to the iPod, iPhone, and a remarkable host of innovations.

Was Jobs aggressive? This is the fierce competitor who attacked Dell for making "un-innovative beige boxes," but his decisions were made with calculation and deep reflection. He not only took the time to arrive at a vision of what people wanted, he also had the courage and patience to set up the system that could deliver it. For Jobs, that meant beginning with the customer experience—"what incredible benefits can we give to the customer?"—and then working backwards to the technology. A less patient leader might have taken an easier, speedier approach by starting with the available technology and then thinking about the marketing and user experience.

As exceptional a leader as he was, Jobs is an abstract figure, a myth to most of us. So, take a few minutes to think about a couple of favorite leaders who were in your life at some point. Consider their history and choices, how they interacted with others. Peel away the layers, and you will see courage underneath. Your favorite coach, teacher, boss—odds are they were deeply courageous and patient. They probably surrounded themselves with others who were courageous and patient, too, people with the willingness and capacity to endure difficult and disagreeable circumstances to achieve their goals. People who consistently chose the hard right over the easy wrong.

Like Jobs, the courageously patient leaders you're thinking of were likely quite patient. They saw the big picture and were methodical about achieving goals. Teaching children a new concept, building a winning sports team, hitting a milestone in your market all require courage, patience, and a proven system. Courageous leaders, as I noted, do not simply reside within a system; they step back from it, lift up, and at some point, remove, prioritize issues, problems, and opportunities and take action. The Seven Critical Needs force team members to step out of the system and courageously assess everyone's role, including their own, as well as the organization's overall purpose.

Courage and patience mean defining every job in a business very clearly. Exactly what responsibilities attach to those qualities? How is performance measured? This takes serious time and effort. Attracting the team members to fill those jobs who positively align to the first critical need—to belong—can also be difficult. Do they have the necessary skills? If not, where exactly are they lacking and can they develop them? The first need also asks: Do they belong in terms of the organization's core values? Do they embrace the foundational beliefs that guide behaviors and decision-making? The second need—to believe—challenges team members if they believe in the company's mission, its reason for existence, and the means it has chosen to pursue its mission. If not, we need to possess the courage to repel them.

The courageously patient organization that has taken the time to create positive alignment on these needs now has a trusted team member it can lead rather than a supervised employee it merely manages. Leaders can be courageous with the employee because goals, accountabilities, and metrics are clear, and effective communication has been built into the system. The employee who has embraced positive alignment feels greater security and trust in the organization, is clear on exactly what she needs to be doing and thinking, and can pursue goals with courage and patience. Attaining positive alignment regarding the seven needs requires courage and patience, but when everyone on the team is there in the affirmative, courage and patience are part of the organization's DNA.

Not everyone will arrive at or be able to positively align. Eliminating those who are a poor fit—because they don't share core values, because they simply don't have the right skills or aptitude, because they aren't passionate about the company's mission—can be tough. Square pegs have a way of becoming entrenched in round holes and throwing up all manner of smoke screens to hide shortcomings. But repelling the poor fits builds a reserve of institutional courage and patience. Poor fits breed fear, destroy courage, and slow the tempo for everyone. Unloading them creates a steady beat for the entire team. Repel them now.

## Rhythm Builds Courage, Patience, and Trust

Courageous patience has a beat, a solid rhythm. Leaders start to hear it and feel it in their bones as they build it into an organization's core. *Tuesday is the day we talk about big issues. We might not mention them much during the rest of the week, but Tuesday's meeting is reserved for the big stuff . . . Monday mornings we review sales numbers . . . Once each quarter we spend a full day digging into our strategic plan . . .*

The ideal meeting structure varies from company to company, and I'll explore meetings in more depth later, but they are a great example of both the rhythm that courageous patience establishes and the bird's-eye view it demands. Businesses need what Michael Gerber, author of *The E-Myth*, calls *in* meetings and *on* meetings. An *in* meeting covers "the old company"—daily operations, last week's numbers, this week's challenges—all the stuff that involves leaders working in the business. An *on* meeting covers "the new company"—improvements to process and people, adjustments that take us to the future. These allow leaders to work on the company, not just in it.

Every organization needs a regular rhythm of both *in* and *on* meetings, and it needs to challenge these meetings and their rhythms by rising above the system. Why is the meeting called that? Should it be renamed to improve focus? Who is in it? Why? What's the goal? Courage and a good business operating system prevent meetings from proliferating and drifting, and it can be the difference between having team members leave the room feeling frustrated and numb or having them leave feeling that they have clarity and have had their voices heard.

The degree of courageous patience in an organization shows not just in the meeting schedule but in the way it conducts them. The cowardly, impatient meeting is top down and overdetermined. Attendees aren't always sure what type of meeting they're in or how it maps with the organization's *why*. For these and other reasons, including everything from the wording of the agenda to the tone and body language of leaders, attendees might be reluctant to speak up, take a chance, or make a mistake. The courageously patient meeting gives all team members a chance to lead with their ideas. It makes room for dissonance, dissent, and mistakes. Consider a gaggle of geese deciding where to land. There's a whole lot of honking and clatter before a decision is made, but then they move there together as a group.

For the geese to land, for team members to feel comfortable, there must be a high degree of trust. Earlier, I noted that defining jobs clearly, including accountabilities and metrics, and getting teammates to understand and embrace *yes* on the first of the Seven Questions—*Do I belong?*—builds Lencioni's "vulnerability-based trust" and Amy Edmondson's "psychological safety"—made popular by Google's Project Aristotle. In fact, all of the Seven Critical Needs do, which is why the courageously patient organization reaps the benefits of deeply felt trust. The employee who knows exactly what he's responsible for, how he's measured, and how he's heard, is not afraid to speak up, whatever the idea. He is also not afraid to say: *I don't know, I need help,* or *I screwed up.* He's not afraid to say: *That's actually not a part of my job; it's yours.* He is *not afraid to debate* and enter into what Brené Brown, in *Dare to Lead,* calls a "rumble"—"a discussion, conversation, or meeting defined by a commitment to lean into vulnerability, to stay curious and generous . . . to be fearless in owning our parts, and . . . to listen with the same passion with which we want to be heard."

Later, I'll explore in greater depth organizational trust and the model I call EATT—evolve, adapt, trust, try. Team members must have a basic level of trust in order to try—not just show up and check boxes, but actually apply their creativity and full abilities to achieving goals. That sort of trying throughout an organization becomes a powerful force. It is part of why some organizations are so adept at evolving and adapting, while others ply the same ideas and methods right into extinction.

A thriving business needs a constant stream of good ideas and useful information to evolve; courageously patient organizations create an environment where both can thrive. It not only provides leaders with snapshots of particular moments in time, but its openness also attracts and gathers data that allows for better decisions. Courageous leaders are constantly collecting info, and they have the systems in place to respond to it nimbly when the time is right. Think of the courageous leader as having a total awareness of the game. He or she is always taking aim, always on point, and continually assessing: *Do I take the shot, do I take the shot . . . ?*

A military concept known as the OODA loop is helpful here. The acronym stands for observe, orient, decide, act. The construct was developed by military strategist Colonel John Boyd for combat but is often referenced in business these days. People sometimes misunderstand the cycle, however, by focusing only on rapid reaction. In Boyd's view, the second *O*, for *orient*, was the most important part of the cycle. A team leader or member must have the courage and patience to orient himself and the organization, to process what is observed, filter it through experience, and test it against objectives before deciding and acting.

Those who misinterpret OODA as being primarily about speed get trapped in an impatient cycle we might christen the OR loop—*observe, react*—which proves every bit as leaden as it sounds. Making bad decisions quickly weighs an organization down; make enough bad decisions fast enough, and the organization races to extinction. Going through every part of the cycle and taking the time to *orient* ultimately provides agility and leads to decisions that are smart and as fast as they need to be. As the Navy SEALs are fond of saying, "Slow is smooth and smooth is fast." Rushing to get things done inevitably leads to errors and confusion that slows the organization down. Having the patience to do things right the first time allows the organization to pick up speed as it moves forward. It's understandable that the vital second *O* of the OODA loop often gets short shrift. As Henry Ford said, "Thinking is the hardest work there is, which is the probable reason why so few people engage in it."

*As Henry Ford said, "Thinking is the hardest work there is, which is the probable reason why so few people engage in it."*

An English friend of mine, Paul McKee, refers to the impatient, those engaged in the OR loop, as "busy fools," and Paul does not suffer fools well. In a conversation one day, he described a particular company as "just a bunch of busy fools." I laughed and asked what he meant. "You know," he said in disgust, "busy, busy, busy. Those people who are always rushing around, never taking time to think." For some in business, everything is urgent and needs to be done yesterday. People with this mindset mean well and are working hard—often too hard and on the wrong things. They confuse urgency with importance. Courageous patience is the filter that allows us to isolate the truly important and go after it in a considered, methodical way.

Courageous patience is a big idea with many facets. We hope that in this section we've clarified what we mean by "courageous patience." Here are a few more reflections:

- Courageous patience is something you have when you are working inside your "Unique Ability." Borrowing from strategic coach Dan Sullivan, *How the Best Get Better* defines Unique Ability as the essence of what you love to do and do best.
- Courageous patience is a mental and physical manifestation of mastery, often called wisdom.
- Courageous patience can be calm.
- Courageous patience is proactive, a willingness to be present and in the moment.
- Courageous patience focuses on the important—not everything should be urgent.
- Courageous patience is creative, not reactive.
- Courageous patience is the opposite of panic.
- Courageous patience is the manifestation of clarity.
- Courageous patience comes when you know what you want and are focused on it.
- Courageous patience can be aggressive in going after a problem or opportunity.
- Courageous patience takes the time to do the hard work and hard thinking, to make the hard call.

- Courageous patience approaches, fear avoids.
- Courageous patience controls passions, providing the courage to slow down and think.
- Courageous patience means being aligned, accountable, authentic, and aware.

I will return to that last point and what it means to be *aligned, accountable, authentic,* and *aware*—the four *As*—later in the book.

I will also return to the following idea, which readers should hear in the high voice of that famous strategic coach from another galaxy:

**Yoda voice:** *"With courage and patience comes consistency; with consistency comes stamina; and with stamina comes amazing, repeatable results."*

The courage, patience, psychological safety, and BITE you create by making and keeping your Seven Promises must be nurtured and protected carefully against things that trigger fear in our human coworkers. All the work we do to help individuals get positively aligned with the seven can be thrown away with a wrong word or wrong action. It takes years to build trust and only seconds to lose it. In the following chapter I will share a couple of psychology-of-fear models with you so you can be aware of the neurological why and some triggers you might trip and traps you might inadvertently step into.

# CHAPTER 3

## Getting *SCARFed*

**WHY DO THE** Seven Promises work so well?

The Seven Promises empower your people, they flip the script, create teamwork norms, close gaps, force precise language, and build BITE, safety, courage, and patience by shifting and then holding leaders and team members in what Daniel Kahneman, winner of the Nobel Prize in economics, calls "System 2 thinking." Kahneman explains that "System 1 thinking" is fast, automatic, intuitive, emotional, fear based, and often *irrational*. He points out that it is the easy, *lazy* path. System 2 thinking is courageous, analytical, logical, *rational,* and difficult—the hard path.

Kahneman became the father of behavioral economics—quite a feat for a psychologist—partly as a result of his surprise at discovering how most economic models assumed that people were rational. Psychologists have long known that much of our thinking is instinctual, fast, irrational, and driven by bias, yet thinkers in economics and business often started with the idea of humans as driven mostly by rational, analytical thought, a view now widely discredited. For survival reasons, the human brain and body have evolved to conserve energy whenever possible. As a result, humans are typically lazy and fearful; they prefer to take the easy way, which is often irrational.

| System 1 Thinking | System 2 Thinking |
| --- | --- |
| Irrational decisions | Rational decisions |
| Fast | Slow |
| Easy | Hard |
| Based on biases, stereotypes, perceptions | Based on facts, realities |
| Happens when alone or with the herd or the mob | Happens in groups, tribal meetings |
| Fear driven, absence of trust | Trust driven, happens when trust exists |

System 1 thinking can be useful as Kahneman points out in *Thinking, Fast and Slow*. It's what gets your foot to the brake when the truck in front of you blows the stop sign at a busy intersection. It's the thinking that puts you on guard when you hear a loud noise, and it supplies the answer when someone asks: What's two plus two? It is also the kind of thinking that protects the status quo, rejects new ideas and methods, and makes people more likely to act in order to avert a loss than to achieve a gain. System 1 thinking is the realm of habit and stereotype. Of particular interest to us, Kahneman argues that System 1 thinking tends to substitute an *easier* solution for a more difficult one whenever it can. Bluntly, it is lazy and often absolutely wrong when it thinks it is right.

System 2 thinking is complex and difficult. It requires stepping back, rising above the processes in place at an organization, thinking and deliberating about things that might be taken for granted or rarely considered. Our stereotypes and biases are mental shortcuts that are lazy, requiring no courage or patience. We should not be surprised that they guide so much decision-making—often under the guise of rational thought—since they avoid the difficult courageous work of true analysis and deliberation.

Thanks to Kahneman, we could alter the earlier Henry Ford quote to read, "*System 2 thinking* is the hardest work there is, which is the probable reason why so few people engage in it." Everyone in your organization is thinking throughout the day, but a surprising amount of that thought is lazy, impatient, uninformed System 1 thinking.

> **"System 2 thinking *is the hardest work there is, which is the probable reason why so few people engage in it.*"**

The Seven Critical Needs demand System 2 thinking, which also leads to consistent and predictable promise keeping. The seven are tough, not lazy or based on biases. Patience, courage, and deliberation disappear when team members are negatively triggered, becoming led by System 1 thinking. During a retreat at the Edward Lowe Foundation, Dr. Dino Signore turned us on to the thinking of David Rock, who has worked on the application of neuroscience to leadership and published a helpful neurological model in "Managing with the Brain in Mind" that is a simple reminder of the negativity triggers we must avoid and the traps we can fall into.

Every new encounter, Rock argues, activates the little brain, which wants to avoid danger and gain reward. A new assignment or new team member at work is no different than a movement in the bush or a shadow at the mouth of the cave was for our forebears. Neurons are activated and hormones—cortisol or oxytocin—are released as we assess whether an event represents an opportunity for reward or a threat. As soon as we sense danger, the fight-or-flight response kicks in and the little brain takes charge.

The threat response is powerful. Rock cites research showing that our perceptions of the way others treat us trigger the same primal neural responses that drive us toward food and away from predators, and experiments suggest that feelings of being rejected socially provoked the same brain activity as physical pain. The threat response diverts oxygen and glucose from other parts of the brain, making analysis and problem-solving difficult just when it's needed most. Humans have a deep need for acceptance. In earlier times, being rejected from the group meant near-certain death at the hands of freezing temperatures, starvation, or saber-toothed tigers. While most of us no longer face the threat of physical death if we are rejected socially, our System 1 brain still treats every social encounter as a life-or-death situation. People who don't have psychological safety at work cannot perform their best.

The reward response, on the other hand, allows the little brain to stand down and makes space for more sophisticated System 2 thinking. Rock has identified the five qualities that activate the basic reward and threat circuitry in the brain. He uses the helpful acronym SCARF to describe this dynamic:

**S**—Status concerns our relative importance to others.

**C**—Certainty is the degree to which we can predict the future.

**A**—Autonomy is our sense of control over decisions in our work and lives.

**R**—Relatedness is the degree of trust and empathy we feel with others.

**F**—Fairness is the perception of impartial, just treatment.

Picture, as Rock says, something comfy, warm, and protective wrapped around the head and neck, and you'll get the idea of SCARF for team members.

Leaders who pay attention to these five qualities can minimize the threat response of the little brain and maximize the reward response. When people feel that their status is secure, they have an idea of what's coming, they have some control over decisions, they trust those they work with, and they are treated fairly; they have the security to engage in more sophisticated and creative thinking and analysis. Remember the people we described previously whom my friend Paul McKee calls "busy fools," constantly rushing around, with no patience and no time to think? That sort of siege mentality often stems from an organizational culture that does not meet members' SCARF needs and unwittingly encourages System 1 thinking.

I'm a fan of the SCARF model because the physiological piece of it makes perfect sense to anyone who has watched a team member wither under a harsh performance review, get micromanaged, or suffer a blistering attack in a meeting. We have all seen people "get SCARFed," and nothing destroys buy-in, inclusion, trust, and engagement faster. (I'll use this verb throughout—*to SCARF* is to trigger a threat response by diminishing someone's status, certainty, autonomy, relatedness, or fairness.)

The other reason we like SCARF is that it dovetails perfectly with the Seven Critical Needs. The critical need *to belong* has everything to do with feeling comfortable in terms of status, certainty, and relatedness. Fairness is only possible if you understand and embrace what you are accountable for, how your work is measured, and how you are heard. We'll come back to SCARF and make more connections as we explore the Seven Critical Needs because it's a helpful model at times, but we want to stress that if you are getting to positive alignment on all Seven Critical Needs, you're meeting your people's SCARF needs too.

|  | Belong | Believe | Accountable | Measured | Heard | Developed | Balanced |
|---|---|---|---|---|---|---|---|
| Status | ✓ | ✓ | ✓ | ✓ | ✓ | ✓ | ✓ |
| Certainty | ✓ | ✓ | ✓ | ✓ | ✓ | ✓ | ✓ |
| Autonomy | ✓ | ✓ | ✓ | ✓ | ✓ | ✓ | ✓ |
| Relatedness | ✓ | ✓ | ✓ | ✓ | ✓ | ✓ | ✓ |
| Fairness | ✓ | ✓ | ✓ | ✓ | ✓ | ✓ | ✓ |

Positive alignment with each of the Seven Critical Needs builds trust, helps people approach and engage, and feel comfortable to engage in System 2 thinking to create. They may even experience joy or love as they help solve issues and help the tribe. On the other hand, negative alignment builds fear, triggering avoidance, shallow System 1 thinking reactions, and stress—things that often lead to anger, hatred, and even attack. I remember the Yoda line from *Star Wars*: "With fear comes anger, with anger comes hatred, and with hatred comes much suffering." It is our job as leaders and managers to build trust through positive alignment.

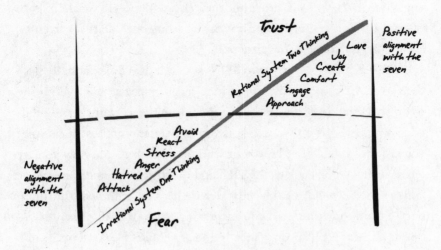

The positive/negative alignment, fear/trust arrow visualizations below help us to understand how the models overlap, complement, and fit together. Key point: the Seven Critical Needs address all the triggers, and the Seven Promises eliminate SCARF triggers, creating psychological safety and always work for you to keep the triggers at bay.

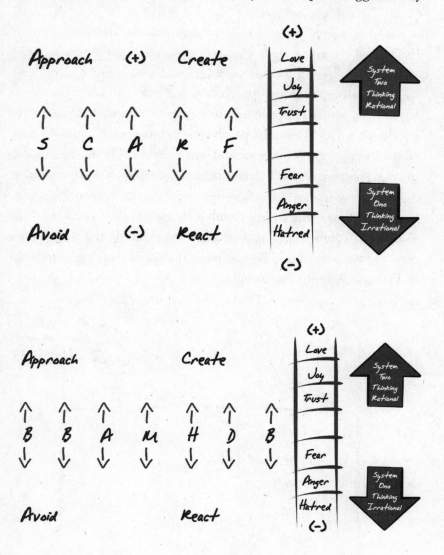

When the Seven Critical Needs are met, when we achieve positive alignment as an organization, the game slows down, fear takes a vacation, and the noise and drama fade away, manifesting as courage and patience—courage and patience to think things through, to have honest debate, to make hard decisions, and to battle through difficult times. The work to achieve positive alignment starts and ends with senior leadership by first defining the organization's definition of each critical need, turning them into promises, and then measuring and constantly working to be sure we keep our promises and maintaining positive alignment through the tools of our BOS.

In this chapter I introduced you to a concept of SCARF and how my clients turn this word into a verb. When a team member gets SCARFed by a teammate or a situation, they can fall into fear mode, and that fear mode can rob them and the entire organization of positive alignment, courage, and patience—System 2 thinking in the blink of an eye. SCARFing someone, or allowing yourself to become SCARFed, removes the courage and patience it takes to maintain one single organization. We will focus on one of my guiding beliefs in the following chapter: *An organization is a fiction and the words we use, the language we use, plays an important role in maintaining one single organization.*

# CHAPTER 4

# Language Matters—
# One Single Organization

**AN IMPORTANT REASON** for the word "culture" in the subtitle is that it emphasizes structure, cohesion, and interaction—not products or services. It emphasizes people. The Seven Critical Needs and Seven Promises are about how people come together to fulfill a common purpose. Without their people, organizations are fictitious and exist only on paper.

One of my guiding belief statements is this: An organization is a fiction, a fiction that is only given meaning and power by those who buy in. If we have 400 people, and 201 buy into this and 199 buy into that, then we have two organizations, not one, and we have already been divided and are on our way to being conquered. We must create and maintain one single organization to compete at a championship level.

We measure how close we are to one single organization through the Seven Question BITE Survey and the BITE Index Report. A high BITE Index score means our people are positively aligned with the Seven Critical Needs. They are highly connected and aren't being routinely SCARFed. A low BITE means our people are negatively or neutrally aligned with the Seven Critical Needs, don't feel connected, and are often SCARFed at work.

In his popular and controversial book, *Homo Deus*, Yuval Noah Harari argues that much of mankind's dominance on Earth comes from an ability to organize around shared meaning. Consider the great organizing principles of human societies, things like money, borders, religion, and national identity. They are useful only because groups of humans have *decided* they have meaning, Harari writes. Once people buy in and organize around such shared beliefs, great things become possible—complex economies, empires, technology, revolutions.

Language itself marks a turning point in this phenomenon of "intersubjectivity," a fancy word for social or shared meanings, closely related to the idea of consensus. We all must agree on definitions in order for our language to work, and once we do, we all make unparalleled progress through the ability to record and transfer knowledge, to communicate complicated thoughts and concepts. Another shade of meaning for "intersubjectivity" has to do with the transfer of feelings or energy from one person to another. We've all experienced this when we're laid low, SCARFed by someone else's bad mood, or have our days lightened by a colleague's infectious good humor.

Intersubjectivity gets to the root of what organizations are—and why they fail. If an organization can achieve great things, it can also implode if its shared beliefs grow hazy or its shared purpose becomes unclear. When an organization does not convey clear core values, a clear purpose, clear accountabilities, clear measurements, clear listening channels, clear opportunities for development or caring around balance, if it harbors people who don't buy in or align positively with the seven, then dysfunction quickly follows.

When humans form into groups, they can solve very complex problems, as long as they can agree on how they name the problem and the words and language around the problem. Words and precise usage of language are the keys to solving complex problems and staying focused. If someone on your team will not agree to the words of the organization—what we call things—then that person does not believe and will destroy efforts to attack issues, ultimately holding the organization back. They must be repelled.

Once you establish the language of your organization around the Seven Critical Needs, it will act as a canary in the coal mine. I had a client in the residential solar business, 300 people with a very sharp, experienced CFO. As part of the seven installation, the senior leadership team agreed that the company would refer to employees as teammates. The term reflected the attitude of the founders and owners and really meant something to them. Yet, the CFO refused to use the term, even argued when called out that "employees" was a better word and she did not buy into the word "teammate." The canary was not chirping in the room when she was there. She would have scored as negative alignment to the critical need *to believe*. As we installed the seven and started surveying and having open conversations around the Seven Critical Needs and keeping the promises, her light bulb lit up and she realized she could not align to the company's definition of the Seven Critical Needs and self-selected out. She was repelled.

The weak links, folks who negatively align to the Seven Critical Needs on a team, not only turn in subpar performances, they also infect their teammates and the entire organization. The intersubjectivity that has allowed humans to rule the earth allows for a crippling transfer of negative energy too. We've all experienced the way that one person's bad attitude or lack of conviction can affect even the most enthusiastic team players. If enough people stopped believing in money, it would soon become simply paper and the economy would crumble. When people don't believe in the same borders—think Cyprus, Northern Ireland, the Middle East—tensions rise and hostility, even war, can break out.

Like money and political systems, an organization is a fiction, only given meaning and power by those who believe in it. If some members don't believe, the organization suffers. If enough stop believing, it disappears.

> **"An organization is a fiction, only given meaning and power by those who believe in it."**

Often, the team members who don't buy in are hard workers with good intentions, or at least, they started out that way. If leaders don't clearly communicate the beliefs at the heart of the organization's existence or, worse, the leaders preach values and principles that they don't practice, team members lose faith. Leaders might fail here because they themselves are hazy on the true purpose and core values, apart from some dusty, awkwardly worded mission statement, or they might know the *why* but have not spelled it out in meaningful ways.

It's no accident that the first two of the Seven Critical Needs are *to belong* and *to believe*. These are existential statements in the truest sense. For the organization, they force the clear definition of core values, every role, "seat," or job, as well as its *why*. The words must be agreed on, written out, and communicated clearly to the entire team. For team members, the first statement—to belong—asks not only if they have the necessary skills for a particular job but, more fundamentally, if they share the organization's core work values. The second critical need statement—to believe—spells out the organization's purpose and asks team members if they are motivated by it and the strategies leadership is using to achieve it.

If we do not get positive alignment around these two fundamental needs, we risk infecting a team with malignant members who don't belong or don't believe in the mission. But the danger runs even deeper. Without belief, the team runs the risk of extinction. They can grow meaningless over time, just as other shared human constructs— Zimbabwe's currency, the Cornish language—lost their relevance when people ceased to believe in and belong to them.

Individual critical needs statements three and four are:

**To be accountable:** I understand and embrace the purpose of my job and roles that make up my job. I know what I should be thinking about and doing and why.

**To be measured:** I understand and embrace how and why I am measured, and I know what constitutes a good job. My measures give me direction and help me to form strategies to fulfill the accountabilities of my job and roles.

It's tough to believe deeply in a purpose, a cause, or a *why* if you're not sure exactly how you are supposed to be contributing (conveyed as accountability) or don't have a fair mechanism for getting feedback (measurement) on those contributions. Has the organization communicated both accountability and measurement clearly, and is it listening to team members' reactions? How closely are leaders listening to team members overall? If team members feel they are not being heard, they are misaligned to the critical need to be heard and, like the canary story, they stop chirping. The *heard* critical need statement, *I understand and embrace how and when my organization listens and how my opinion is heard*, clearly puts the burden on the shoulders of organizational leaders to define and then stick to how the company listens.

The final two statements focus on key benefits and effects of the organization on team members' lives:

**To be developed:** I understand and embrace my organization's development mechanisms and how I can develop; I know how to take an active role in my own development.

**To be balanced:** I understand and embrace my organization's definition of balance and the mechanisms I can participate in to reach my goal of balance.

These two statements imply that the organization has a plan based around clearly defined goals for development and balance.

The Seven Critical Needs coupled with Seven Promises offer the clearest way to get and maintain shared belief in an organization. They are the best mechanisms to leverage language—the most powerful human example of shared meaning—to achieve incredible results.

## Just Semantics? It's All Semantics!

A common response at this point is that what we are arguing is "just semantics." But when it comes to precise language, Mark Twain believed that "the difference between the almost right word and the right word is really a large matter. 'Tis the difference between the lightning bug and the lightning."

Does it matter whether team members call those who come to your organization "customers," "clients," "users," "members," or something else? Of course. In ways subtle and not so subtle, that label will shape every interaction they have. The difference between the motto Apple rolled out in 1997, "Think different," and IBM's motto, "Think," was a small, merely semantic difference, a single word that signified an innovative philosophy, billions in profit, and ultimately, market dominance.

Not only does semantics matter, *it's all semantics*. Recall our argument that an organization is essentially a human fiction, only given meaning and power by those who believe in it. If that's the case, what happens when things aren't named correctly and consistently, or when team members use conflicting language to describe things? When one team member sees something as a "motto," another as a "guideline," a third as a "slogan," and a fourth discounts it as mere cheerleading, that doesn't just mean poor cohesion within the organization. You have four people *believing* four different things. Since the organization quite literally is its members' beliefs, you have four different organizations.

P. J. Fleck, head football coach at the University of Minnesota, is passionate about the power of shared language. So passionate, in fact, that he created a glossary of terms to pin down exactly what the most important words and phrases in his program mean. For example, success is "peace of mind which is a direct result of self-satisfaction in knowing you did your best to become the best you are capable of becoming" (borrowed from John Wooden), and energy is "the place where passion and purpose collide." F.A.M.I.L.Y. is understood by all to mean "Forget About Me, I Love You." The team glossary has over 80 entries. Fleck's players and coaches all speak the same language and believe in the why and how of their one, single organization. And it is for that reason, being one single organization that speaks the same language, players will tell you, that they've beaten so many more talented teams during their time at Minnesota.

We typically get eight answers when we work with senior leadership teams and ask eight team members: *What is the purpose of the organization?* When we ask about accountabilities, measurement, and how opinions are heard, we also get as many answers as there are respondents. Setting strategy, achieving goals, and building crack teams at one organization is difficult. It's impossible when you have eight disparate organizations, conflicting fictions, housed under one roof.

To solve a problem, people must first name it and agree on the language surrounding it. Doing this well is not easy, and it's not merely a pro forma step. Language reflects thought. Sloppy, impatient language reflects sloppy, impatient thought. The Seven Promises provide a path to courage and patience through clear thought that produces accurate, specific language for everything from an organization's overall purpose to how the Tuesday meeting gets named.

In chapters 6 through 12 we will dive into the yin and yang of each critical need/promise combination. But first, in chapter 5, let's take a look at the up-front work you and your team will need to create and agree upon. Once the Seven Critical Needs and Seven Promises are working in conjunction with our BOS, via insights from your BITE Survey and BITE Index, you can constantly measure and improve your organization's health. When you inspect what you expect and believe that what gets measured gets done, the Seven Question BITE Survey and BITE Index will tell when and where you are becoming divided and where you can take action to reinforce and maintain one single organization forever.

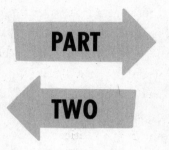

PART

TWO

# Exploring the Seven Critical Needs and Promises

# CHAPTER 5

# Needs, Promises, Measurement, Action

**IN PART II,** we will explore what each of the Seven Critical Needs entails, its benefits, why it works, where organizations tend to fall short, and how getting positive alignment builds BITE, courage, and patience. The first two needs—*to belong* and *to believe*—are foundational and by far the most important. The next three—*to be accountable, to be measured,* and *to be heard*—are primarily about communication and return us to the point of precise language. They involve everything from reflecting on how meetings are named and structured to clearly stating the purpose of the organization.

The last two needs, about *development* and *balance,* involve everyone's favorite radio station, WIIFM—What's in it for me? They are vital for buy-in, loyalty, and engagement. They help team members who can get to positive alignment see that their values and goals align with the organization's.

Each critical need has two parts that manifest as Critical Need Statements. The organization must complete the first statement before it can prompt team members to consider the second statement. We'll give concrete examples along the way and explore the effects of not attaining positive alignment. Our exploration of each critical need chapter ends with an exercise, diagnosing courage, patience, and BITE, which will help you assess just how close to positive alignment your organization already is and how much work needs to be done.

The Seven Critical Needs are intimately intertwined and overlap in many ways. Team members can't agree with how they're being measured (need four), for instance, if they don't know what they're accountable for (need three). It's easier to determine if you have or can develop the skills your role requires, as need one asks, and if you have a sense of your development path within the organization, covered in need six.

Positive alignment to these Seven Critical Needs cuts confusion, fear, and mistrust. It creates an environment of clarity and accountability in which individual contributors can see the organization's *why* and *where*, its strategic vision, and connects that future to their own as they work, inspired to make both a reality.

Bryan Bunker, the COO of Noël Group, argues that the Seven Promises work partly by inspiring ICs—individual contributors—to form an emotional connection to a company.

"If you can get to a point where people belong and believe, where they understand what they are accountable for, how they're measured, heard, developed, and balanced I feel like you're putting your arms around the entire individual and not just saying, *'Do you come to work on time and do your job?'*" Bunker says. "You have to show compassion for the entire individual. We're all complex, as human beings. We have interests, loved ones, hobbies. We have emotional hot buttons and we have strengths. If you don't acknowledge that in some way, there's never really an emotional connection to the business, and people won't give you their discretionary effort. To me, that's a really important part of leadership—unlocking discretionary effort."

Unlocking discretionary effort—that is, getting to positive alignment on the Seven Critical Needs—requires courage and builds this quality for both the IC and the organization.

Making and keeping the Seven Promises based on the Seven Critical Needs is an ongoing process, not one and done. Attaining and maintaining positive alignment takes constant effort. The first step in becoming a courageously patient organization with BITE, though, involves building an awareness of the kinds of gaps we have been talking about. How courageous is your organization? How far are you from positive alignment on each question?

## Systemize Your Promise Keeping

"If you systemize the predictable you can humanize the exceptional."
— Isadore Sharpe, founder, Four Seasons hotels

Our favorite metaphor for a business operating system (BOS) is the waterwheel. Powering human endeavors for millennia, from quaint millpond waterwheels that grind flour to the turbines at the base of hydroelectric dams, a waterwheel is powerful, steady, patient, courageous, always aligned, and versatile. With proper tending and maintenance, they are unfailingly consistent, essentially running on their own, with great torque and momentum, powered by a renewable source—water. Instead of water, your wheel is powered by your people, team members who aligned with your definition of the Seven Critical Needs and have accepted and helped you keep your Seven Promises. Your waterwheel or turbine is your BOS.

Like a waterwheel, a good BOS powers your organization. It captures the source of an organization's energy and direction, and with a little maintenance, it, too, runs on its own. The Seven Critical Needs and Promises are the buckets on that wheel. If you can use an effective BOS to consistently align and fill your Seven Critical Needs buckets with positive alignment, you will harness incredible energy.

A BOS provides an efficient, repeatable way for businesses to clarify exactly who is responsible for what and to prioritize and focus the company's limited resources against its vision. A BOS has a concrete set of tools that help owners set priorities, review team members, track numbers, and most of all, communicate. They often include other tools that help leaders develop marketing strategies and set aside time to plan, following a detailed timeline and agenda.

Every organization has some sort of BOS, whether leaders know it or not. When we ran our sailing gear dot-com, Layline, we had various systems, procedures, and tools that together formed an organic operating system. It did the job and mirrored elements of today's popular systems, but a lack of understanding of our own methods was a drawback.

You might ask, "If our existing tools work, why does it matter if we see them as part of an operating system?" Well, for starters, it's rare to find an organic BOS with no gaps or weak spots. Seeing your tools in the context of one fully integrated system helps you to spot the holes and plug them or adopt a more thorough system. You also want the various moving parts complementing each other, not working at cross-purposes. Seeing your BOS holistically facilitates that effort, which is especially important as a business grows. The same tools and systems that worked great when the office had 15 team members won't work when there are 750, or likely even 25. Many of my clients hire me as they're expanding because the old systems and tools no longer cut it.

Lee Walker, the millennial CEO of Walker Auto & Truck mentioned earlier, became our EOS client when his company grew from 100 to around 700 employees. It was managed during that expansion by a growing number of active family members he jokingly calls "the cousin consortium."

"We got to a point in our growth where we had a higher need for structure, for leadership talent, and teamwork, and acknowledged that we weren't going to be sustainable if we didn't evolve in our capacity to run a bigger organization," Walker says. "When I describe EOS to people, I say, if you're successful, you've probably thought about many of these things, they're already part of your philosophy. But it's about creating the structure for discipline, adopting something you can utilize consistently, perpetually, without backsliding."

One advantage of the prepackaged business operating systems available today is that they come with a complete set of clearly articulated tools. There's less guesswork and fewer gaps—or at least, that should be the case. A solid BOS should assure that you consistently communicate, maintain, and refine how folks align positively to the Seven Critical Needs. A solid BOS makes and keeps your promises for you. If it does not, it might have terrific features, but the gaps will hurt the organization. Doing the hard work, what we call the *heavy lift*, of defining the "first positive alignment" is baked into a solid BOS like EOS. Choosing the right BOS depends on the needs and personality of your organization.

Most of our coaches work with the Entrepreneurial Operating System (EOS), which we think is extremely effective at maintaining seven positive alignments. Other business operating systems include 4DX, Gazelles/Rockefeller Habits/Scaling Up, the Advantage, Holacracy, Pinnacle, and System & Soul. Some call the OKR process out of Google a BOS, but we think it is just one piece of a good BOS. All of them have some excellent features.

By understanding the concepts in this book, you will be able to use the Critical Needs to BOS Tools Matrix tool included in the resources section. This tool is a rubric that maps and measures the effectiveness and fit of your BOS with the Seven Critical Needs. When considering a BOS, I encourage you to use the matrix, which I delve into further in the next section. Beginning there will help you as you browse their offerings to see if one of these systems is right for you. We have some examples and have done some of the matrix work for you.

You might also determine that the system you have developed organically already does this work. If that's the case, we hope that the following chapters on each of the critical needs will help you keep the buckets on your waterwheel full. Whatever the gaps between the initial dream you had for your organization and the way it has actually grown, your BOS probably plays a role.

An effective BOS builds courage, patience, and measurable BITE, and it offers an incredible competitive advantage, but installing one is not easy. In our experience, it takes eighteen months before the system begins to yield the kind of BITE we are encouraging, and full implementation takes around three years. Someone at the organization needs to own the BOS and oversee this effort, since owners typically can't devote the necessary time.

And, of course, there will be resistance.

Every problem at an organization, at root, is a people problem, and even engaged people resist change. The resistance put up by those who aren't engaged, who don't belong or believe in your core values or purpose, will be even greater. This is another reason that the Seven Critical Needs and Seven Promises are vital whether or not you decide to install a new BOS. Inviting everyone in the organization via your Seven Promises to get aligned with positive alignment on believing, belonging, accountability, measurement, hearing, development, and balance fills the buckets of whatever system is powering the organization. Eliminating those who can't or won't align with positive alignment honors and empowers those who are engaged and builds courage for all.

Once you determine what positive alignment looks like for all seven, the practical tools of your BOS keep you there, turning a powerful, patient, courageous waterwheel that provides its own momentum and the kind of competitive advantage that leaves the competition floundering in the outflow below your dam.

## Is Your BOS Up to the Task?

Does your business operating system have the ability to address the Seven Critical Needs and then systematically make and keep your Seven Promises?

We run our clients through an exercise where they discover if their BOS has the tools and chops to deliver on the Seven Promises. The tool we use is called "the BITE Mapping Guide."

It is pretty simple. We ask them to write the Seven Critical Needs across the top and then list the tools from their BOS down the left side. Then we ask them to break into pairs and put a check mark in the matrix cell where the tool enables the individual to get to positive alignment.

The normal takeaway when they do this as EOS clients is: "We do not need any more tools to make and keep our Seven Promises. We just need to use the tools we have."

For instance, the V/TO (Vision/Traction Organizer) in the y-axis is the document in EOS where your strategic plan is outlined and your core values and core focus are detailed. People see from the V/TO what your core values are (to belong) and see your focus and entire plan (to believe). In the V/TO they are able to imagine a future for themselves, which informs their growth ideas (to be developed). GWC means *get it*, *want it*, and *capacity to do the* it; it = job and roles.

We work with many companies that are not running on a pre-packaged BOS. One of our facilitations is to walk them through an understanding that they have tools and rhythms in place that address the seven. We do this using the BITE Mapping Guide.

# BITE MAPPING GUIDE
## FOR COMPANIES RUNNING ON EOS®

| Your Business Operating System Tools | Belong | Believe | Accountable | Measured | Heard | Developed | Balanced |
|---|---|---|---|---|---|---|---|
| V/TO™ | ✔ | ✔ | | | | ✔ | |
| CORE VALUES | ✔ | | ✔ | | | | |
| ACCOUNTABILITY CHART™ | ✔ | | | ✔ | | ✔ | |
| GWC™ | ✔ | | ✔ | | ✔ | ✔ | ✔ |
| PEOPLE ANALYZER™ | ✔ | | ✔ | | ✔ | ✔ | |
| SCORECARDS | | ✔ | ✔ | ✔ | ✔ | ✔ | |
| ROCKS | | ✔ | ✔ | ✔ | ✔ | ✔ | |
| MEETING PULSE™ | | | | | ✔ | ✔ | |
| LEVEL 10 MEETING™ | | | | | ✔ | ✔ | |
| IDS™ | | ✔ | | | ✔ | ✔ | |
| 5-5-5™ | ✔ | ✔ | ✔ | ✔ | ✔ | ✔ | ✔ |
| LMA™ | | | | | ✔ | ✔ | ✔ |
| | | | | | | | |
| | | | | | | | |
| | | | | | | | |
| | | | | | | | |

BITE7™
BUY-IN | INCLUSION | TRUST | ENGAGEMENT

WWW.BITE7.COM

*Tools listed are the intellectual property of EOS Worldwide.*

## Promises Require Shared Effort

The work of finding positive alignment to the critical needs is not all on you or your leadership team's shoulders. Remember, we are doing this for our people and not to them. We are giving them the gift of our Seven Promises, and they are accepting the gift. It is a two-way street, and each of the seven has different levels of ownership effort.

The "Effort Arrows" diagram illustrates the relative ongoing effort that is owned by the organization and the individual.

## Effort Arrows

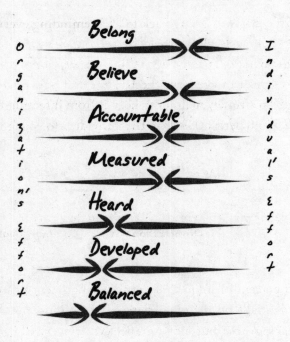

*The arrows relate to the Seven Promises by showing the relative amount of ongoing work the organization puts in (arrow on the left) and the amount of ongoing work the individual puts in (arrow on the right) to attain and maintain positive alignment to the Seven Critical Needs.*

We have two sides, the ongoing effort required by the organization and the ongoing effort required by the individual unique to each promise. Note: The percentages change from one organization to another, so do not take this as universal, but the numbers I include here represent relevant ranges. I briefly dive into each of the seven arrow pairs.

## Belong

| Organization 80% | Individual 20% |
|---|---|

The effort of constantly going back to and reminding everyone what it means to belong is mostly held by the organization, leadership, and management. It is the duty of the organization to keep this promise, to screen to keep out the bad fits and to purge/prune the "dead wood" in a timely manner to keep it from infecting the whole. Much less (say 20 percent) is up to the individual to engage and work to belong.

## Believe

| Organization 80% | Individual 20% |
|---|---|

Around 80 percent of influencing positive alignment on the critical need *to believe* falls on the organization, which must not only articulate a clear purpose but also an effective strategy, showing every accountability level, for realizing it. Many organizations solve part of that equation, the why or the how, but leave the other half untended. It is up to the individual to put in 20 percent to understand and align with the plan.

## Accountable

Organization 65%    Individual 35%

Clearly defining and communicating what needs to be done when someone takes a job is the work of the organization. Yet, in the Seven Promises model, we have hired people who belong and believe, and we want their opinions on how they can fulfill the purpose of their job and roles. We want to open the door. Thirty-five percent of the load is on them to understand and embrace their accountabilities.

## Measured

Organization 65%    Individual 35%

We need to be super clear and define how success is measured, yet we want to keep the door open for our folks to add refinements to how they are measured. Tommy might be motivated by X, while Janna is motived by Y. If both X and Y get us to Z, does it matter? We must apply common sense.

## Heard

Organization 30%    Individual 70%

This is where the script flips and the load is on the shoulders of the individual. We cannot force a person to speak up or share their thoughts or opinions. Yet, we can be super clear and consistent on how and when the organization listens and responds. We must be clear about when listening channels are open. And then we must be consistent. We are asking: *Do you understand and embrace what we do here?* We are not Mr. Spock—we cannot and are not tasked with mind melding with every individual.

## Developed

| Organization 20% | Individual 80% |
| --- | --- |

Not everyone really wants to develop. Sometimes they are fine knowing what they know. But the organization must be clear, precise, and consistent in how it opens the door for development and helps people step through.

## Balanced

| Organization 20% | Individual 80% |
| --- | --- |

The responsibility rests on the shoulders of the individual around 80 percent of the time. This is an area that needs to be incredibly systemized through your BOS. How are you measuring and looking for balance? Does the individual know this is how, when you are asking them about work-life, finances, and wellness? Do they understand how they step into the conversation, how they pull the alert button, how they help themselves? Honor them by being super clear, consistent, and precise when it comes to balance—the organization owns 20 percent.

## Your Senior Leadership Team's Role in Alignment

There I sat, a bit frustrated and disappointed, reviewing the latest BITE Index scores from one of my client's BITE7 Surveys. They were not up to par, and this was reflected in their financial statements, which I was reviewing at the same time.

My thoughts were: *Damn, they have invested so much time and money, and they are still stuck.*

And then I recalled the wisdom of Don Tinney and Gino Wickman:

"Walt, remember, as the leadership team goes, so goes the rest of the organization."

The 800-person family business had segmented the BITE7 Survey to align with business units tied directly to senior leadership team seats. The poor scores indicated that family members were not in the right seats and were not buying into EOS, BITE7, or the Seven Promises.

Across my 200+ client teams I know what a healthy senior leadership team (SLT) looks like, I see how they grow, I see how they behave and treat each other, I hear how they communicate. This team was still not healthy. How could anyone think that the people who work for these leaders could be expected to align positively to the Seven Critical Needs when it was clear the SLT was not healthy or aligned around them either?

The "organizational health" Promised Land I write about here in *Attract or Repel* is directly tied to the senior leadership team's health. The path does not go around them; it goes through them.

Most of my client teams start out as dysfunctional and confused, which leads to poor health and cohesion. In 90 percent of the cases, one or two team members need to be repelled before team health will rise. Doing EOS well will shine a clear light on who these people are, and they will either self-select out or the CEO will have to make the hard call and weed them out.

If you have a couple of leaders on your team who do not belong, do not believe, are not accountable, don't hit their measures, squelch how people are heard, do not take an active role in helping develop others, and just don't care about balance, then you do not have a healthy team and, as they go, so goes the rest of the organization.

Organizational health starts with the senior leadership team.

## The BITE Survey and the BITE Index— What Gets Measured Gets Done

How well are you keeping your promises? We subscribe to the saying: "What gets measured gets done, and you must inspect what you expect." We believe strongly in the necessity of measuring anything we are trying to maintain or improve in order to communicate. Measurement is a strong form of communication.

If you are familiar with business guru Peter Drucker, you have likely heard two of his most famous quotes: "What gets measured gets managed" and "Culture eats strategy for breakfast." If you agree with both of these statements, then you might be thinking something like: *I don't know how to measure my culture, so I'm not managing it, and if I don't manage our culture, no matter how strong our strategy is, one of our competitors out there who is measuring and managing their culture is going to eat us for breakfast.* Don't worry, dear reader, the solution is at hand.

One thing our clients have in common is they believe in the importance of culture, taking care of their people, and fostering robust organizational health, but how to measure and manage culture and organizational health can be unclear. Culture may be the most important factor in the success of a business, as Peter Drucker asserts, but it is largely subjective, and it can be difficult to measure things that are subjective.

That's where BITE7 comes in. By assigning scores to your people's experiences—measuring the degree to which your BOS is meeting their Seven Critical Needs—you will have a reliable way of diagnosing problems and prescribing solutions based on data.

You measure every aspect of your business in order to identify and manage operational inefficiencies, so why not apply the same principles of measurement to your organization's health?

A helpful way to think about the importance of measuring and managing your organization's health is through the analogy of medicine. It takes years of medical school and residency to become a doctor. And years more to achieve mastery in a given field of medicine with the experience and intuition to hypothesize with reliable accuracy a patient's health problem after a conversation in the examining room. And yet, despite all of this experience, a good doctor is not going to make an official diagnosis based on assumptions alone. A good doctor doesn't make a diagnosis until he or she collects the appropriate data by *measuring* things like blood pressure, pulse rate, respiratory rate, and body temperature. More serious cases may also require swabbing the throat, drawing blood, or putting the patient through an MRI or CT scan.

Not until they've measured all of the relevant markers and analyzed the data will the doctor make an official diagnosis and devise a plan of treatment. And once the treatment begins, the doctor will continue to measure the key indicators to see if the plan is producing the desired improvements or if it needs to be adjusted.

Because you're concerned about your physical health, you will see your doctor for routine physicals for the rest of your life. You don't want to be caught unaware by a problem that could be potentially fatal if left untreated but is easily treated if diagnosed early. Smart leaders use the exact same approach to organizational health.

If you want to manage your organization's health—its culture—you have to measure it.

## The Three Traps

The BITE7 Framework avoids the three traps that snare many engagement or trust programs.

- **To them, not for them.** BITE7 flips the script. One of the reasons trust programs fail is that employees see it as being done to them and not for them. Your promises flip the script: *for*, not *to*.
- **Not simple and consistent.** BITE7 is simple and consistent. Another trap is a combination of overactivity: too many surveys, and the questions are always changing. This confuses our people, and they default to thinking: *to* me, not *for* me. You keep it simple with one seven-question survey.
- **No systematic way to establish baseline and respond.** BITE7 is rooted in actionable response. The third trap is an inability to establish a baseline and respond. You get data but you don't have a way to systematically respond. With BITE7, you use the BITE Index and you respond via the tools of your BOS that you map using the BITE Mapping Guide.

The BITE Survey is a short seven-question survey that walks team members through their alignment to the Seven Critical Needs Statements as questions. The survey asks them to answer each on a simple 1 to 10 scale. Folks who answer 8, 9, or 10 are positively aligned, those who answer 7 are neutral, and 1 to 6 responses are not aligned, negative. This is a great way to kick off the initiative with team members, gauge how much work lies ahead, and begin forming a strategy. We offer this survey online for you to use at BITE7.com.

# SEVEN QUESTION BITE SURVEY™

**For each of the 7 questions**, you will be asked to consider **several critical factors**. Take a little time to think about each, determine which factors are most important to you, then come up with a score. Don't stress out. **Trust your gut feeling**. Scores are mandatory for each question. Written feedback is optional, but **we strongly encourage you to explain your scores**. Your explanations are what allow us to have the clearest idea of what's working and not working so that we can come up with a tailored plan to make the organization stronger and your work experience better.

**Instructions:**

- A score of **1** means you are answering the question with the strongest "**No!**" possible.
- A score of **10** means you are answering the question with the strongest "**Yes!**" possible.

| 1 = NO, NOT AT ALL | | | | | | | | | 10 = YES, ABSOLUTELY |

### DO I BELONG?
*I understand and embrace my organization's core values, and I have (or can develop) the skills my job demands.* ***I belong.***

| 1 | 2 | 3 | 4 | 5 | 6 | 7 | 8 | 9 | 10 |
|---|---|---|---|---|---|---|---|---|----|

COMMENTS:

### DO I BELIEVE?
*I know and believe in my organization's Why. I also believe in our leadership, my teammates, our strategic direction, and the products or services we provide.* ***I believe.***

| 1 | 2 | 3 | 4 | 5 | 6 | 7 | 8 | 9 | 10 |
|---|---|---|---|---|---|---|---|---|----|

COMMENTS:

### DO I UNDERSTAND AND EMBRACE WHAT I'M ACCOUNTABLE FOR?
*I understand and embrace the purpose of my job and the roles that make up my job. I know what I should be thinking about and doing and why.* ***I am accountable.***

| 1 | 2 | 3 | 4 | 5 | 6 | 7 | 8 | 9 | 10 |
|---|---|---|---|---|---|---|---|---|----|

COMMENTS:

### DO I UNDERSTAND AND EMBRACE HOW I'M MEASURED?
*I understand and embrace how and why I am measured, and I know what constitutes a "good job." My measures give me direction and help me form strategies to do great work in all of my roles .* ***I am well measured.***

| 1 | 2 | 3 | 4 | 5 | 6 | 7 | 8 | 9 | 10 |
|---|---|---|---|---|---|---|---|---|----|

COMMENTS:

### DO I UNDERSTAND AND EMBRACE HOW I'M HEARD?
*I understand and embrace how and when my organization listens and responds.* ***I am heard.***

| 1 | 2 | 3 | 4 | 5 | 6 | 7 | 8 | 9 | 10 |
|---|---|---|---|---|---|---|---|---|----|

COMMENTS:

### DO I UNDERSTAND AND EMBRACE HOW I'M DEVELOPED?
*I understand and embrace my organization's development mechanisms and how I can develop; I know how to take an active role in my own development.* ***I am developing.***

| 1 | 2 | 3 | 4 | 5 | 6 | 7 | 8 | 9 | 10 |
|---|---|---|---|---|---|---|---|---|----|

COMMENTS:

### DO I UNDERSTAND AND EMBRACE HOW I MAINTAIN BALANCE?
*I understand and embrace my organization's definition of balance and the mechanisms I can use to reach my goals for balance. (Three components of balance: 1. Work-life, 2. Compensation, 3. Health and Wellness.)* ***I am balanced.***

| 1 | 2 | 3 | 4 | 5 | 6 | 7 | 8 | 9 | 10 |
|---|---|---|---|---|---|---|---|---|----|

COMMENTS:

## The BITE Index

Defining exactly how we measure buy-in, inclusion, trust, and engagement with the BITE Survey and then boiling that down to a single simple number is where the magic lives in the BITE7 Framework. Measuring helps communicate both the why and how we will take action to honor your Seven Promises is critical.

Do you remember the H-shaped BITE Index Graph and the statistics around how one negatively aligned individual offsets a positively aligned individual in chapter 3? Our organizational power comes from our positively aligned teammates; the BITE Index represents in one single number the net power of our culture overall. The BITE Index report is your window into the BITE power of your company, providing you with a clear road map you can use to communicate, work on, and measure. It provides you with a consistent rinse-and-repeat baseline tool. You survey, you review your BITE Index, you create a plan on how to leverage the tools of your BOS, you communicate the plan using the BITE Index report, you act, then you measure again. Consistent, actionable, repeatable, and simple.

## Buy-In, Inclusion, Trust, Engagement Report

Compare your courage to others via the BITE Index.

# BITE7™ Report

| Average | Question | Index |
|:---:|:---:|:---:|
| 9.30 | I Belong | 78 |
| 8.93 | I Believe | 61 |
| 9.26 | I'm Accountable | 74 |
| 8.80 | I'm Measured | 54 |
| 8.70 | I'm Heard | 54 |
| 9.02 | I'm Developed | 67 |
| 8.67 | I'm Balanced | 50 |

| BITE7 INDEX™: | 63 |
|:---:|:---:|

*Buy-in, Inclusion, Trust, Engagement*

**BITE7 INDEX™ Key**

| -100 to 50 = Weak | 51 to 69 = Average | 70+ = Strong |
|:---:|:---:|:---:|

| 🗣 DISENGAGED | 😐 NEUTRAL | 🙂 ENGAGED |
|:---:|:---:|:---:|
| 15 | 90 | 217 |
| *5%* | *28%* | *67%* |

| Total Respondents | 46 |
|:---|:---:|
| Total Responses | 322 |
| Average | 8.96 |
| Report Date | 6/23/2023 |

Now that we have our heads around the effort arrows, the three traps, the BITE Survey, and the BITE Index, it is time to dig into each of the Seven Critical Needs Statements to understand how much work is involved before you can administer your first BITE Survey, receive your first BITE Index Report, and get ready to roll out your first Seven Promises plan. Starting in chapter 6, we dive into each of the Seven Critical Needs, cover the work that needs to be done, expand on what each need means, and finish each with a diagnostic you can use to understand how much work you need to do to satisfy each and get ready to make and keep promises.

# CHAPTER 6

# To Belong

> ## Critical Need 1. To Belong
>
> **Organization Statement:** We have clearly defined our core values and have mechanisms in place to hire, reward, adjust, and fire around them, and we have defined all skills necessary for every job and role.
>
> **Team Member/Individual Statement:** I understand and embrace my organization's core values, and I have (or can develop) the skills my job demands. **I belong.**

**WHY IS THIS** critical need the first and most important of the Seven Critical Needs? Well, we began this book by talking about the dream behind the birth of every organization. The kind of people that entrepreneurs envision surrounding themselves with make up the heart of that dream. Stuffed into the gap between the dream and the soulless machine companies so often become are people who don't belong—the negative wedges that break our courageous organization apart.

Nothing sucks more energy from an organization or destroys BITE, courage, and patience faster than people who do not belong. Entrepreneurs don't imagine collecting such people, but they creep in over time and, in the worst instances, become organizational terrorists, holding hostage the team members who belong. Getting positive alignment to this critical need is the most important step in becoming a courageous organization.

After I started my first company, employees who had been around a while sometimes brought up "the speech" I gave when I hired them. At first, I wasn't sure what they meant—in most ways, they were more aware of my leadership style back then than I was—but when I thought about it, I realized that there was a consistent rap I delivered to potential hires during the interview process. One such interview with a former member of the Harvard sailing team, nicknamed "Chief," went something like this:

> Chief, your qualifications look terrific. You did well at Harvard and you have great experience sailing. You seem like you would be a perfect fit, but before you say yes, I want you to think about some things. Consider what I'm about to say, sleep on it, and make sure you understand it. Every day when you walk through that door, I want you to bring a positive, cheerful attitude. I do not want to be surrounded by a bunch of Debbie Downers. That does not mean ignoring problems or pretending. I expect you to be cognizant of each situation too. You need to get serious when the situation demands it, but typically, we want to operate in a positive and cheerful manner. Also, we value listening here. We strive to really understand each other, our customers, and our vendors, and

one way we do this is by trying to always ask three questions first, especially with customers. With the best of intentions, people often want to give customers input without having the full picture. We avoid this by attempting to ask three questions before we answer one. You'll learn more about this over time. Be sure to ask Henry and others for their take on it as you continue your interview rounds. We believe that the only dumb question is the one you don't ask. This ethos is important enough that we have an acronym for it around the office, PC3: be positive, cheerful, cognizant, and ask three questions first. I also want you to challenge your work. Try to understand why you're doing something, and if it seems off, say, "Doing it this other way would make more sense." If you are PC3 and challenging your work, you'll be a great team member. Everyone will love you and you'll excel here.

This was my "attract or repel" speech. You may have a similar interview rap, though like me at my first company, you might have spent little time reflecting on it. The roots of this speech and my acronym, PC3, actually go back to my college years. It was then that I decided that these were three qualities I valued. I wanted to be positive, cheerful, and cognizant, and even at that young age, I realized that I wanted to surround myself with people who were "PC3" too.

My whole rap about being positive, cheerful, and cognizant; asking customers three questions first; realizing the only dumb question is the one you don't ask; and continually challenging your work all boils down to the first of the Seven Critical Needs: *to belong*.

Getting to positive alignment on the critical need *to belong* would have given our core values teeth and integrated them into every facet of the organization. This, in turn, would have fostered more patience and courage by weeding out those who did not belong (the worst courage and patience destroyers), clarifying accountabilities, and providing a touchstone against which strategy could be measured. *We're faced with a tough decision. Okay, well, let's think about how each possible choice maps with our core values, our belief, and our roles.* Additionally, weeding out the bad fits before hiring them would have saved us the considerable amount of money we spent finding, hiring, and training their replacements.

Along with the rest of the Seven Critical Needs, getting to positive alignment on *I belong* as individuals and as an organization would have been a key component of building the sort of decision matrices we mentioned in part I, a hallmark of any courageously patient organization.

Like many entrepreneurs, we were in the neighborhood on this and many other fronts. Did we have core values? Absolutely. But we did not integrate them fully or have our ideal team because we were not asking the right questions.

For both the organization as a whole and individual team members, attaining and maintaining positive alignment on the critical need *to belong* takes serious work, but the payoff is hard to overestimate. If every problem is at bottom a people problem, think of the enormous number of problems that get solved or prevented simply by having people who belong. Doing the difficult work of maintaining positive alignment on this critical need has exponential benefits, creating a snowball effect that lets you roll right over the competition.

This critical need also tops the list because it addresses one of our most fundamental needs as humans, right up there with finding food and avoiding danger. We evolved as tribal creatures, and the need to belong is powerful because for millions of years our lives depended on it. As we mentioned, research suggests that social situations—a meeting, performance review, presentation—can trigger the same primal threat response as an attacking bear.

Sadly, those who don't belong can live with the threat response almost continually activated, as they get SCARFed again and again and fall back into System 1 thinking. Those who do belong are comfortable with their status, certainty, autonomy, and relatedness and believe they are treated with fairness. This gives them the security and confidence to analyze honestly, take risks, think creatively, admit mistakes, and be friendly with fellow team members even during fierce debate. They are free to engage in System 2 thinking. Later, I will help you assess whether your BOS actively attracts those who can maintain positive alignment and repels those who can't.

Team members who attain a positive alignment answer to the critical need *to belong* are courageous and contribute to deep reserves of courage in the organization. They are courageous with fellow team members because they aren't worried about their status, certainty, and relatedness. They are courageous with leaders because they feel good about the levels of fairness and autonomy they're being shown. And if they are getting to and maintaining positive alignment on the rest of the Seven Critical Needs, too, they are able to take the long view and think deeply about problems and goals.

Recall our discussion of leadership and management in part I. Management is about daily needs—sales numbers, new equipment, filling a missed order—and working *in* the business, as Michael Gerber, author of *The E-Myth*, says. Leadership is about the big picture, strategy, and working *on* the business. Those who don't belong must be managed. They spend their days scratching items off the never-ending to-do list that managers feed them. Managing is difficult, time-consuming, and impossible to scale.

Team members who belong can be led. They are given a task, ask a couple of clarifying questions, and then complete it without oversight. As soon as they do, they're back, saying not only, "Hey, what's next?" but also, "I was thinking about this." People who belong and who are led share in the burden and excitement of higher-level thinking with leaders, and they free up the leadership team to do even more work *on* the business, to stick with Gerber's model, instead of simply *in* it.

One leader's or one department's bad fit can be another's A player. The process starts with leaders finding clarity on values, roles, and skills.

Maybe you feel that your core values already are clear and well integrated into the organization. That might be the case, but in my experience, it's exceedingly rare. At the end of this section, our Diagnosing Courage exercise will help you reflect on your BOS, asking if it helps you to determine how strong your core values are and how far your organization is from enjoying positive alignment on the first of the Seven Critical Needs.

The Diagnosing Courage and Patience exercises also will help you assess how well you have defined each role within the organization— the second key task leaders and teams must complete before they can have team members ask themselves, *Do I belong?* For team members, the first half of this critical need prompts them to assess whether their values align with the organization's. The second part asks them to assess if they have or can develop the skill sets necessary to fill their roles. Aligning with core values is vital, but a software developer who believes in the organization's values and can't write code is in the wrong role. A whiz-bang coder who doesn't buy the overall values can't adequately fill the role either.

You'll note that I use "roles" as a sub-unit of "jobs," "hats," or Jim Collins's increasingly popular "seats" to refer to the various roles in an organization. Like "team member," this term originated with my sports and sailing experience, but after decades of running my own companies and coaching others, we have come to realize it's the most accurate label. A "job" is actually made up of many roles. On offense, I play center and report to the offensive-line coach, while on defense I play linebacker and report to the defensive-back coach. Marketing director is a job label, sure, but at a particular organization, it might include a creative role, a supervisory/mentor role, a client services role, a copyeditor role, and so on.

Team members need to know the purpose and requirements of each role, a more complex and accurate construct in my view than the simple term "job" indicates. Since it's my contention that an organization is a fiction resting entirely on the belief of its members, this connotation of "role" is not just a linguistic trick. It is existential, central to what it means to belong and to believe and, in a very real sense, to create an organization anew each day. "Role" implies that every team member, from the janitor to the CEO, plays a vital role in the organization's survival.

Each role has a particular perspective, and when two roles look at something, you can determine where that something truly lies. In navigation, we call this triangulation: you look at an object and determine a position, or a bearing, and somebody else looks at it, and he or she has another bearing, and together, you can get a precise fix on that thing. This is how our GPS satellites work: they pick up your signal, compare your signal with what other satellites are receiving, do some math, and then deliver a precise location back to your app in a never-ending cycle of precise positioning.

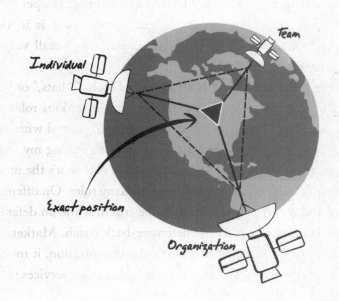

Many of the owners and leadership teams we run into *think* they have already done their share of the work on the first of our Seven Critical Needs and accounted for every role in the organization. They have job descriptions from HR and titles and a classic direct-report org chart. None of this gets you to a solid positive alignment. None of these goes to the level of roles. Forget about titles and jobs, and think about everything that needs to be thought about and done every second of every day. What roles emerge from that exercise? Where's the overlap? What are the gaps? The organization must engage in this process before leaders can ask team members if they belong.

The organization that attains and maintains positive alignment on *to belong* has an incredible gatekeeper for building and maintaining a courageously patient organization. Every role is clear, and the core values it has defined can then be used in recruiting, interviewing, training, measuring, and developing team members. Those core values become an integral part of the decision rubrics that every courageous organization builds into the system: *Of these difficult options, which aligns best with our core values?*

When people problems arise, *to belong* also becomes part of an invaluable checklist, along with the rest of the Seven Critical Needs. There's a problem with Dave? Well, *does he belong? Does he believe? What exactly is Dave accountable for, and does he understand it? Is he being measured well? Has he embraced the agreed metrics?* You get the idea. *To belong* not only becomes the gatekeeper for hiring new people, via the tools of an effective BOS; it makes the difficult conversations down the road much easier because team members have been kept in the loop about core values, purpose, accountability, measurement, and actively involved in asking the key questions related to them.

We keep talking about hard work, and attaining and maintaining positive alignment on the Seven Critical Needs requires plenty, but when coupled with a consistent BOS, this work saves immense amounts of time. Once you have established core values and defined every role, the process of maintaining positive alignment can start to feel magical because your people pick it up and keep it going. Gaps are filled and duplication eliminated as things begin to fall into place. Often, people who don't belong self-select out of the organization once they're presented with clear core values and well-defined roles, saving leaders headaches and tough conversations.

Getting to positive alignment on *to belong* is also *the* key to growth. A client of mine, Sine Tea, provides a good example. The company started small and from the start, made education and sustainability priorities, alongside profits. Partners Bob and Alan were successful and had a completely open-door policy, but as the organization approached 200 employees and expanded nationally, growth took its toll.

Expansion and quality appeared contradictory, as did growth and inclusiveness, sustainability and education. Don, the star salesman, wasn't cutting it as a national sales director. Russell, who had done a great job packing tea, couldn't stay off the line now that he was operations manager. It was hard to tell if Katrina did a good job because when we forgot about titles and began defining roles, no one knew what a vice president of culture and sustainability was accountable for. Alan left the organization and since every driver, packer, and admin still had Bob's ear, he was wearing thin.

Attaining and maintaining positive alignment on *to belong* took care of many of Sine Tea's growing pains, and it did so without acrimony. By working through the Seven Critical Need Statements to gain clarity and then turning those into promises, Sine gave their employees permission to work on alignment. Don asked if he could drop back to being just a great sales contributor—he did not have the skills or desire to gain the skills needed to fulfill some of the roles that were critical to be a national sales director. Now Don is thriving.

Russell ultimately owned the operations manager job as he was able to understand the skills his job and roles required and set a plan to attain and master those skills. Faced with the organization's core values and clearly defined roles, Katrina realized that her deepest values were not really aligned, and her skills were more aligned with those offered by industry involvement than a profitable business. She happily went to work for a trade association, and the organization did not need to replace a fancy title that had no real accountabilities—a job title without roles. Within nine months, other employees who couldn't align to positive alignment self-selected out. Other team members stayed but realized they did not belong in their current roles and worked with management to attain positive alignment. With a leadership team that was now positively aligned to the Seven Critical Needs, Bob could preserve his sanity and spend more time working *on* the business rather than just *in* it.

Becoming a courageously patient organization gave Sine the ability to maintain consistency and quality during its expansion, and it all started with getting to and maintaining positive alignment on the critical need *to belong*.

## Attaining and Maintaining Positive Alignment on Belonging

The critical need *to belong* ranks first on our list and demands the most work from the organization. It is foundational. Surrounding yourself with people who can enthusiastically say *yes, I belong*, as we have argued, eliminates untold problems and builds courage like nothing else. It is not half the battle; in a very real sense, it *is* the battle.

The organization's leadership must think deeply about, discover, and develop its core values to pave the way for maintaining positive alignment. It must articulate them clearly and integrate them into every level of the organization—and, as author Patrick Lencioni says, "give them teeth." Faced with core values that permeate every strategy, project, and decision, the individual then has to decide if his or her core values align with those of the organization.

Equally important, leadership, with the help of everyone, must do the heavy lifting of defining all *roles*—a task more difficult and useful than that of defining *jobs*—to determine who belongs where, which tasks are falling through the cracks, and what duplication can be eliminated. Once the organization has defined all roles and installed workable architecture, it can decide, along with team members, if they have or can develop the skills necessary to truly belong in the roles they occupy.

## Core Values

Discovering, or uncovering, your organization's core values and communicating them consistently and clearly is half the work of positive alignment on the critical need *to belong*. We began this book talking about the dream that is the seed from which every organization grows. Core values are the manifestation of and prerequisite for that dream, like the owner who pictured her business long before she started it saw herself surrounded by people who shared certain values, people she liked, people who belonged. In terms of the waterwheel we described at the start of part II, core values are the axle at the very center (yep, the *core*). Collectively, they are the thing that makes the waterwheel work, the backbone of momentum, the point where everything— including courage—comes together. They guide long-term strategy as well as small, quick decisions, and they are one of two key criteria in deciding who belongs.

Test your results against our earlier discussion of core values. Make sure your list doesn't include distant goals or aspirations, skills, or what Lencioni calls "permission-to-play" values (honesty, integrity, etc.). Most of all, make sure that the values you end up with are sincere and unique to your organization. Authentic, clearly articulated core values will fire up the troops and build cohesion and courage. Hollow "values" that smack of a marketing campaign can result in eye rolls and even disengagement.

Like the end of a good novel, the core values that emerge from this exercise might seem both surprising and inevitable. *We've always emphasized that we want people to enjoy their jobs, so it makes sense that "fun at work" is on the board, but we never articulated the fact that this is one of the four core values this place runs on.* Some of your core values might be a little edgy if that's who you are as an organization. One of my clients lists "no jerks" as a core value. This is something the organization feels passionately about, and it expresses the attitude in passionate terms. That's fine. Core values are for internal use. If authenticity demands colorful language, quirky phrasing, humor, or a dash of vitriol, go for it.

## Give Your Core Values Teeth

You've established your core values. Now what? At many organizations, core values are a one-time exercise. They're named hastily, printed on a plaque somewhere or mentioned at a retreat, and begin to rot. That's unfortunate but understandable. Truly integrating your core values into the organization, making them the touchstone for who belongs and how decisions get made is painful. The process requires deep reserves of courage. It puts new pressure on leaders and holds them and team members to higher standards. Some, you will quickly see, cannot find positive alignment on belonging. They will have to be let go, or as often happens, will realize themselves that they can't achieve positive alignment and self-select out. Repel.

If you take core values seriously, though, and use them to underpin positive alignment on belonging and the rest of the Seven Critical Needs, you unleash a force that would impress even Obi-Wan Kenobi. They become a key factor in *leading* rather than merely *managing*, as we discussed in part I and elsewhere. Since virtually all problems at an organization are people problems, using core values alignment for positive alignment on belonging eliminates endless problems before they are born. Imagine the power of an organization where everyone belongs and is aligned with the core values. Imagine the courage that gets built by having this consistent lens through which all strategy and decisions are viewed.

If you have not attempted to implement core values until now, understand that the effort won't be realized overnight. In our experience, it takes six to eight months of hard work for the initiative to take root. During that time, your core values should become a part of all hiring, planning, and strategizing. They should be present in meetings and memos, the backbone of collaborative efforts. Leaders should demonstrate clearly that core values aren't slogans but a decision matrix. *If we choose X or decide Y, how does that align with our core values?*

Team members will begin to use core values to make their own decisions, too—at least those who belong will. Those who can't reach this degree of alignment need to go.

Those who belong and are aligned to your core values will feel more engaged, even inspired, by your ubiquitous core values. Make them a part of all training and training materials, all conversations, onboarding, and measurements. Use them to recruit, hire and fire, attract and repel.

## Promises Are Created by an Act of Will

Very few moral judgments are more intuitively obvious and widely shared than this: ***Promises are made to be kept.*** Making and keeping promises takes patience and courage; for most of us they are not entered into lightly. This is the power we are trying to harness and why it bears repeating from chapter 1.

A feature of promises that makes them interesting to us as we build an intentional culture is their role in producing trust, trust that facilitates social coordination and cooperation.

As business owners, we don't think much about the connection between promises and our organizational health. We understand contractual and commercial promises, but we often overlook the advantages we could harness if we applied the same amount of rigor to our cultural promises.

Unlike everyday moral duties—the duty to not steal, for example—promises are not owed equally to everyone, but, rather, only to those whom we have made a promise. Further, promises are voluntary; we don't have to make promises, but we must keep them when we do.

Promises are created *by* acts of will. When I promise to do something, it means that, by doing so, I have created the obligation to do it.

The idea that we simply manufacture promissory obligations by speaking them, like an incantation, is a decidedly mysterious and powerful feature of promises. As David Hume remarked in *A Treatise on Human Nature*:*

---

* Emphasis in the original.

> I shall further observe, that, since every new promise imposes a new obligation of morality on the person who promises, and since this new obligation arises from his will; it is one of the most mysterious and incomprehensible operations that can possibly be imagined, and may even be compared to *transubstantiation* or *holy orders*, where a certain form of words, along with a certain intention, changes entirely the nature of an external object, and even of a human creature.

## The Interview Promise

Ask a dozen job candidates if they are positive, cheerful, and cognizant, and you'll get a dozen yeses. Few will answer: *No, I'm actually fairly dour and unaware.* Instead, put your core values out there so strongly during all interviews that they become a promise to new hires:

*John, I am making a promise to you, the same one I make to everyone who works here: I am going to surround you with people who share core values. Let me explain them for you. They are x, y, z. Now, if you have these values, our organization will be heaven for you, nirvana. If not, it will be hell on earth. You'll be miserable, everyone around you will be miserable, and before long, I or the organization will flush you out. Does this sound like a fair promise?*

Hopefully, this approach should become part of your BOS.

Once someone is hired, they need to be regularly asked to reaffirm that they belong.

*You did an excellent job on project X, which demonstrates this core value. However, you're slipping in this other area, which shows a lack of alignment with our core value of . . . Which value do you think you are struggling with? Which one is your strongest?*

EOS offers advice and systemizes this tactic as part of their suggested HR process. If someone is out of alignment with a core value once the implementation is well underway (180 to 270 days in), one must list and clearly communicate at least three examples of this misalignment or you're not likely to be heard. After pointing out the ways that a team member is not meeting the core value standard, give him thirty days to correct course. If he doesn't get it right then, allow another thirty days, but make it clear that continued misalignment at sixty days means that the person does not belong and will be asked to leave.

Integrating core values and making sure team members are aligned with them gets you only halfway to positive alignment on belonging. Employing people with the right skills in the right roles is equally important. At Layline, the most positive, cheerful, cognizant team members would have accomplished little as customer advisors if they didn't have and couldn't develop the basic skills necessary for the seasonal roles attached to that job, such as vendor relations, buying, and HTML knowledge.

As we pointed out, a *job* includes many *roles*, and focusing on them gives you a more thorough inventory than if you only consider mere jobs or titles. People need to be clear on which roles they hold as well as the skills needed to fill them before they can get to positive alignment on the second half of belonging: *yes, I have or can develop the skills necessary for my roles.*

## Diagnosing How Much Work You Need to Do as an Organization

### • TO BELONG •

*Exercise for PBOLTs and Senior Leadership to Answer*

Grab a piece of paper and follow these prompts.

1. Write down your organization's core values.
2. Are the things you wrote down presented systematically during interviewing, training, onboarding, as "core values?"
3. Write down one time during the last two days that you anchored a decision in the organization's core values and framed it to team members using that term.
4. Has your leadership team in the last six months assessed everything that needs to be thought about and accomplished at your organization and summarized these into roles that belong to jobs?
5. Are you engaging team members to ask if they have the needed skills for those roles at least every 90 days?
6. Has all overlap between roles been eliminated, and have all gaps been filled on your list of roles?

After completing the prompts above, review your answers and use the scoring guide that follows to determine how far from positive alignment you are. For each of your answers, give yourself a score from one of the following four choices:

**WAY FAR | MANY MILES | RIGHT AROUND THE CORNER | THERE**

*Scoring Guide*

**How to Score Prompt 1:** *Write down your organization's core values.*

- If doing this took more than 90 seconds, you rate Way Far.
- More than five things noted? That's a laundry list, not core values—Many Miles.
- Only one or two things noted? That's sketchy—Way Far.
- If the language is not clear, simple, and specific (each item ranging from one strong word to a basic sentence), you can probably tell where you stand between Way Far and Right Around the Corner, but There you ain't.

**How to Score Prompt 2:** *Are the things you wrote down presented systematically during interviewing, training, onboarding, etc., as "core values"?*

- If the answer is no, you're somewhere between Way Far and Many Miles.
- If it's yes, you might be There or Right Around the Corner.

**How to Score Prompt 3:** *Write down one time during the last two days that you anchored a decision in the organization's core values and framed it to team members using that term.*

- If you can't, you're somewhere between Way Far and Many Miles.
- If you can, you're probably either There or Right Around the Corner.

**How to Score Prompt 4:** *Has your leadership team in the last six months assessed everything that needs to be thought about and accomplished at your organization and summarized these into roles that belong to jobs?*

- If the answer is no, you're Way Far.
- If it's yes, you're probably There or Right Around the Corner.

**How to Score Prompt 5:** *Are you engaging team members to ask if they have the needed skills for those roles at least every 90 days?*

- If you're not, you're Way Far.
- If you are, you're somewhere between There and Many Miles.

**How to Score Prompt 6:** *Has all overlap between roles been eliminated, and have all gaps been filled on your list of roles?*

- If you said that it has, you're There—and probably lying.
- If it's close, you're somewhere between Way Far and Right Around the Corner.

# CHAPTER 7

# To Believe

---

**Critical Need 2. To Believe**

**Organization Statement:** We know our *why*, our focus, and our strategic direction. We have mechanisms in place to clearly and consistently communicate our strategies for achieving it.

**Team Member/Individual Statement:** I know and believe in my organization's *why*. I also believe in our leadership, my teammates, our strategic direction, and the products and services we provide. **I believe.**

---

**NONPROFIT LEADERS OFTEN** have issues with role clarity and strategy when it comes to executing their purpose, or *why*, but they tend to understand that the organization's overall mission is important, driving loyalty, productivity, and cohesion. They use it to recruit and to interview and to fire up the troops. They know that their *why* is the reason so many talented, motivated people eschew higher pay and benefits to work in the nonprofit world. Team members who care deeply about the environment, social justice, inequality, animal rights—pick a cause—are willing to work long and hard for less pay and fewer benefits because they believe in a particular *why*.

Is there a better way to motivate and focus a team than to highlight to members the greater good they're striving for? Executive directors at nonprofits say *no* without hesitation, but we are always amazed by the number of PBOLTs (private business owners with leadership teams) who have not given their *why* much thought, articulated it clearly, or communicated it to the troops.

Some answer my question above—What better way to motivate and focus?—with a word: "money." To which I say: *Really?* Is that what you want on your tombstone? *She made a lot of money . . . He amassed many dollars.* Is that really what gets you out of bed in the morning or keeps you at the office until midnight when you're immersed in an important project? I ask this as someone who fully understands and appreciates the value of a buck. My team and I started and ran four companies and were driven to make money at all of them. We've spent the last decade coaching leadership teams on strategies that make them more money and help organizations grow the bottom line.

Extra money is a motivator only to the extent that it's critical to peoples' perception of their imagined futures. Beyond that, a sole focus on money conveys that you actually don't give a flip about them or where their lives are going.

The point is: No matter how important making money is, the *why* is more important for most of your team members. Was Steve Jobs motivated by money? He certainly made his share, and we are sure that pleased him, but after his return to Apple, he was paid one dollar a year. He ultimately made a fortune in stock, but his compensation structure proves money wasn't his main motivator. He was driven to revolutionize the way people interacted with technology, to provide superior design and a user experience like no other. That was his *why*, and perhaps because it was so strong, he proved a master at using narrative and gestures both grand and small to motivate his team around a purpose, as well as his strategy for getting there. You could say that his return to Apple in 1997 after the company recorded a quarterly loss of $708 million brought back the *why*—and what a difference that made.

*Okay,* you might think, *the organizational* why *has been a big factor at Apple, where genius developers and designers are working on the next iGadget, but my team? Purpose? Belief?* Yes, your team.

One of my clients has this belief statement: *We believe in the power of listening.* What are they, lawyers, counselors, music producers? No, this is the janitorial supplies distributor I mentioned earlier. They believe that they are a customer-facing organization every single day, and that they find their competitive advantage by truly taking the time to listen to their customers, vendors, and the market. Before they put anything in place, they ask, "Will that make us better listeners?" And while janitorial supplies might seem unglamorous, team members see this mission as a source of pride and loyalty.

More examples of belief statements from my clients include: *Relationships that last forever, Improving the way people make and use energy,* and *Empowering others to accomplish that which they never thought they could.* Each of these organizations learned to motivate team members and shape strategy by getting to positive alignment on the critical need *to believe.*

Recall the Gallup stats we cited in part I, showing that 70 percent of all US workers are either neutrally engaged or unengaged at work. Here's another: "Only slightly more than a third of millennial workers strongly agree that the mission or purpose of their organization makes them feel their job is important," according to Gallup. But focusing on the *why* turns the numbers upside down: 67 percent of millennials are engaged at work "when they strongly agree that the mission or purpose of their company makes them feel their job is important." Only 14 percent of millennials who strongly disagree with that statement are engaged. Millennials are nearly *five times* more likely to be engaged when the organization has a strong *why* they can connect their work to.

Those stats are worth considering, since millennials are nearly 40 percent of the workforce as I write this and could account for as much as 75 percent by 2025, but as I pointed out in part I, this is not just about millennials. They might have a little more courage in pursuing purpose than previous generations, but all team members want to feel attached to a *why* that makes their days at an organization mean something. The desire to be part of some larger purpose is embedded in our DNA, an integral part of what it means to be human. Working together for some greater good—hunting a buffalo or clearing out a cave—was how we survived. The bigger *why* connects us to the tribe, helps address SCARF, and allows us to align personal purpose with organizational purpose.

I don't mean to suggest that focusing on the *why* is about self-sacrifice. Just the opposite. I have coached football players for years because I think it builds character and confidence and teaches important skills to the young men on my teams. But I also take great personal satisfaction from it. Serving that greater good lets me tune in to WIIFM—What's in it for me?—like nothing else.

As we said, this critical need is just as important as *to belong*, and like that first one, the benefits of getting to positive alignment here are immense. Gallup data show that when workers are driven by the larger mission, "companies realize major performance gains, including increased employee loyalty and retention, greater customer engagement, improved strategic alignment, and enhanced clarity about work priorities."

When *why* is clearly articulated and integrated throughout the organization, your *why* allows you to focus and engage in clear System 2 thinking as you allocate limited resources. Like the first critical need—*to belong*—this one becomes a litmus test and a key part of a courageously patient organization's built-in decision matrices. *We're faced with two difficult options here? Okay, which one will best serve our purpose?* A true *why* allows you to simplify and focus, to choose to decide to say firmly *no*.

When we turned our sailing gear catalogue into the dot-com, Layline.com, our purpose stayed the same. It was taking care of the finite days our customers had on the water and protecting their weekends. We were dealing with clients who were passionate about their sailboat racing but very busy, with limited time on the water. We saw their weekends as sacred because of our *why* (weekend days = finite), and so, we never considered putting off a call or delivery of the best equipment until Monday. There was no question about it—call them, ship it overnight, don't worry about the cost, protect the weekend.

As we found at Layline, having a *why* allows you to debate and argue courageously about the *what* and the *how*. Our purpose percolated through daily operations and shaped our workweek. Because we believed in freedom for sailors, we protected their Fridays by delivering the right things on time to the right place. We would include screws and caulk, so they would not have to make a trip to the hardware store, send articles with their packages so they could study and use their gear to its full potential, all without being asked, which meant listening, asking questions, planning ahead, and working a little harder on Thursdays. The *why* wasn't just part of a logo or mentioned annually at a retreat. We integrated it fully into our daily work.

Knowing and leading with the *why* builds courage and allows the big picture to be contemplated. Keeping one eye always on the overall mission means slowing down to work on broader strategy as well as daily needs—*on*, and not just *in*, the organization.

I hope I've made the case for why *why* is important, but I want to caution that we are talking about a true, authentic purpose here. Your *why* can't simply be something posted on the wall, a plaque or platitude.

The second half of getting to positive alignment on *to believe* involves strategy. A *why* is meaningless if the organization does not develop and communicate a strategy for fulfilling it. Team members must get to positive alignment on the strategy as well as the purpose. Those who like the destination but not the route should find their own way—to the exit. Nonprofits, as we mentioned, are often good at getting team members to positive alignment on the *why*, but they often suffer severely from lack of buy-in on the chosen strategy for getting there.

Even a successful, growing organization doing many things well can have real trouble thinking strategically and executing tactically. Growth is difficult, and even with a good leadership team—the place where strategic thinking should live—the future gets neglected unless leaders have a rigorous framework in place for prioritizing the future and figuring out how to get there. Instead, energy and attention get consumed by execution—hiring, training, opening new locations. Fires multiply with each new store, office, service, major client. Who has time to think strategically?

Lee Walker, the millennial CEO of Walker Auto & Truck, is one of the strongest strategic thinkers we know—and one of our best clients. Since 2009 when the company affiliated with NAPA, it has grown from 15 stores and 100 employees to around 70 stores and 700 employees.

"There was a realization that we couldn't just keep going down the same path," says Walker, who, at 40, runs the third-generation family business in North Carolina with the help of keen relatives. "We really needed to educate ourselves and equip our executive leadership team with a better strategy and more support in decision-making—a system for vetting ideas and conceptualizing."

With leaders who grew up in the business and knew it intimately, Walker says, there was no shortage of strategic thinking around ideas at the company. In some ways, there were too many—or too many ideas without a framework to guide and contain them.

"It's been very helpful," Walker says. "We don't make decisions by consensus, but we generally reach consensus, get to clarity and a shared vision because we've done such a thorough evaluation and investigation, debating all those critical elements of whatever it is that we're trying to do. The real long-term strategic vision has been seen through these different filters of thinking and challenging."

Most of all, the Seven Promises, STATE (strategic thinking and tactical execution) framework, which will be further defined in this chapter, and EOS tools have helped turn Vision into Profit.

"All the Walkers can sit in a room and come up with an idea, but if we can't really put some legs on it and execute, then you got nothing," Walker says. "This was where we needed to build up our team."

## A Promise Must Be Accepted

Yale philosophy professor Stephen Darwall writes:

> *A promise's existence is conditional on its acceptance (or at least not being rejected) by the promisee. I simply cannot make a promise to you if you refuse to accept it.*
>
> *In this way, a promise is like a gift; it must be accepted or not rejected to be given at all. Otherwise, I will have no more than tried to promise, or give a gift. Various other rights and prerogatives*

*derive from the would-be promisee's authority to reject the prom-*
*ise. Just as it is part of the very idea of a gift that it cannot be*
*forced on someone, so also does a would-be promisee have standing*
*to demand that he be genuinely free to reject it—that his acceptance*
*not be forced, manipulated, extracted by deception, and so on.*

Attract or repel—thank you, Stephen. This is the point. If someone we are interviewing does not want to accept our promises, then
they should naturally be repelled. The Seven Promises are made *for*
employees who want to accept the promises, who want to be part of
the promises. It is empowering for all sides.

When hiring, leaders use the BITE Framework to promise prospective employees that the organization will run a certain way on
certain core values with a certain mission, accountability mechanisms,
evaluation metrics, listening methods, development support, and safe-
guards for balance, and the prospective employee must thoughtfully
accept those promises before joining the team. It cannot be imposed
on them without their agreement. The Seven Promises should have a
strong attract-or-repel impact on anyone considering joining.

Your Seven Promises are the key to your intentional culture.
Without the commitment and the intestinal fortitude to make promises, we are empty sacks of air and our employees see us as such.

Your Seven Promises set the stage for an individual to belong
and believe in your organization. As they see you keep your promises,
they will begin to feel safe, included, trusted, and engaged. They will
understand where they fit into the fabric of your organization. They
will buy in and flourish. Their efforts will align with the team's, adding momentum to the flywheel and making your organization health-
ier and stronger.

If faith small as a mustard seed can move a mountain, imagine
what an entire team of people who have faith in your organization can

accomplish. Going back to my belief that an organization is a fiction that is only given meaning and power by those who buy in, for people to buy in, to have faith, there can be no gaps in the messaging or data. It is widely understood that when there are gaps in data, humans fill in the blanks with what they believe to be true. It is the duty of leadership to clearly paint the path to the future that aligns with the why. A well-written, simplified, and shared strategic plan will allow you to paint a picture for your people, a picture that takes them into the future and maps a path back to the present, filling in the blanks along the way, a picture that allows them to see themselves in that picture that they believe in. Does your plan make sense, is it simple, can you share it to paint the picture they will believe in?

## Attaining and Maintaining Positive Alignment on Believing

Positive alignment on the critical need *to believe* demands that the organization possess a strong purpose, or *why*, and a clear strategy for achieving it. Team members must then be able to say, *yes, I believe* in that purpose and leadership's strategy for fulfilling it.

If I walked up to you on the street and asked you to hold down a button on a box I was carrying, you might walk away, or you might, running on autopilot, hold it down halfheartedly for a minute or two. But if I told you that releasing the button would blow up the diner on the corner, and you believed this to be true, you would hold that button down until your finger turned blue or you dropped from exhaustion. The menial suddenly has meaning. Do we really need statistics to get it that people are more motivated when they know and believe in the purpose behind what they do? Isn't it just common sense to think that team members work better when they know the *why* that ties those long workdays together?

We all want positive alignment on believing. Greater engagement, loyalty, and harmony for team members might be the most obvious benefit, but having an authentic purpose also allows the organization to focus and set priorities. As with core values, it becomes another key decision matrix. *Should we do X or Y? Well, which one is more aligned with our purpose?* Having a strong purpose allows you to say *no* faster because so many choices will immediately appear at odds with it. A big part of finding positive alignment on this critical need, paradoxically, involves finding no.

Team members who can unhesitatingly say *yes, I believe* are able to take the long view and rise above the daily minutiae to engage in the System 2 rational thinking. In this way, purpose fosters courage on both an organizational and personal level. Around 80 percent of determining positive alignment on the critical need *to believe* falls on the organization, which must not only articulate a clear purpose from senior leadership but also an effective strategy at every accountability level for realizing it. Many organizations solve part of that equation but leave the other half untended.

Our thinking about the second of the Seven Critical Needs has been heavily influenced by Simon Sinek, author of *Start with Why*. Most organizations, Sinek argues, start with the *what*—the widgets they produce or services they provide. Some also focus on the *how*. They can communicate how they do what they do, the qualities or processes that set them apart. Very few, however, have given much thought or space to their *why*. Starting with this inner circle—the organization's purpose—and working outward to the *what*, in Sinek's view, inspires and builds loyalty like nothing else. He calls these three concentric rings (*why, how, what*) "the Golden Circle" and encourages leaders to start in the center.

Apple is a prime example of a company that starts with *why*. Sinek argues that Apple's *why* is the belief in challenging the status quo. Apple's *how* is that they think differently; its *what* is changing the way people interact with technology. This is no small part of why consumers used to line up for city blocks to get the latest Mac gadget the day it was released. Apple's *why* inspires some of the top engineers and designers in the business as well as a customer base whose brand loyalty looks a lot like a religion.

The stated purpose of Starbucks is "to inspire and nurture the human spirit—one person, one cup, and one neighborhood at a time." There's no mention of top-quality coffee beans or superior roasting methods. So, breaking this down, the *why* is to inspire and nurture the human spirit; their *how* is one person, one cup, and one neighborhood at a time; the *what* is comfortable seating, eclectic music, pleasant lighting, Wi-Fi, and friendly baristas. Working outward from the stated purpose, it's easy to see why. Comfortable seating, eclectic music, pleasant lighting, Wi-Fi, and friendly baristas are every bit as important to Starbucks as quality coffee. The local Starbucks is meant to be a community hub where people work, read, meet, and talk—and drink various beverages in cups. Starbucks' *why*, which is printed on the inside of employees' green aprons, so they see it every day, is unique and guides activity and decision-making from the board room to the baristas.

At Layline our belief was: *We only have a finite number of days on this earth: protect them.* Our *how*: *Protect our customers' finite weekends/ days off.* Our *what*: *By carrying the latest and the best, shipping it out fast, and guaranteeing our work 100 percent.* We ate it if we missed a delivery date. While we did not know this was a golden circle statement, it was our guide for everything we did. If we were pondering a course, or found ourselves reacting to a situation, we could run it through this filter and come to a consistent decision.

A large industrial rigging client's *why* is: *Working together safely.* How? *By delivering high quality, on schedule, cost effective work.* Its *what*:

*Relationships that last forever.* All of their decisions pass through this filter, and it is baked into their BOS.

If you can get to a strong *why* or belief statement, your center, filling in the *how* and *what* are easy. Here are belief/why statement examples:

- We believe retail is not dead; as a matter of fact, it is very much alive.
- We believe in the power of listening and taking action.
- Partnering with companies to offer the right balance between technology and people. Balance.
- Leading people to financial security.
- Why: Delivering repeatable wow experiences. How: Making sports accessible, safe, and enjoyable for people of all experience levels.
- Through constant never-ending improvement of our mind, body, character, and spirit, we will enable ourselves and each other to excel. We are essentially in the people development business.
- We believe in empowering others to accomplish that which they never thought they could.
- Sound is nurturing to one's soul.
- Seniors deserve more. *How?* Access to a diverse innovative group of services. *What?* Enabling them to live safely and comfortably in the residence of their choice.
- Helping with our unique knowledge and capabilities.
- Improving the way people make and use energy.

Positive alignment on believing begins with the organization's leadership team thinking deeply about its *why* and creating a belief or purpose statement that articulates it. I prefer "belief statements" to "mission statements," which are often wordy and too broad in scope.

Sure, you can start with your current mission statement as a guide. My belief statement is: "I believe in freedom." We can expand that this way "the freedom that comes when owners and leadership teams have the guts to do what it takes to go from good to great, to do what it takes to create a championship organization. When they do this they create freedom for everyone around them, employees, vendors, customers, the world at large. I do this by being a focused Implementer of EOS."

Freedom is my *why*. *How* I achieve it is by being an awesome EOS Implementer. *What* I create is more time, more money, and less stress for clients. Everything I do is filtered against this belief.

A good belief statement is the nut at the center of everything. It should be succinct—just a sentence or two—and clear. It doesn't have to start "We believe," but we recommend beginning with that format as you craft one to keep leaders focused on belief and purpose and not drifting off into the business mission or a distant vision.

## Plan to Achieve Your *Why*

Your BOS should drive your planning and shape your strategy.

Most organizations are no strangers to strategic planning, and each has its preferred methods. After Jim Collins and Jerry Porras published *Built to Last*, their notion of the BHAG (big hairy audacious goal) became popular as a way to focus on long-term ambitions. Other approaches offer different names for that long-term goal and the near-term strategies needed to achieve it. Many find Franklin Covey's notion of scheduling the "big rocks"—your top strategic priorities—rather than sorting through gravel helpful. Google's OKRs (Objectives and Key Results) have gained popularity as a planning tool too.

We like the critical success factor method to strategic thinking, a method pioneered by D. Ronald Daniel of McKinsey & Company and advanced through MIT's Jack Rockart in the 1960s. A vision statement—see your belief statement—is supported by a list of the critical success factors (CSFs) that must manifest for the vision to be realized. These are typically the things that need to be in place by the end of the year for the plan to stay on track. Beneath each CSF are one or more goals or targets that help fulfill the vision in smaller steps. Beneath each goal are one or more strategy statements—mini-plans laying out how we accomplish the goals—and finally, beneath them, the tactics or to-do items that allow us to execute the strategy.

Here is an example of the STATE model we teach:

| **S**trategic | **T**hinking | **A**nd | **T**actical | **E**xecution |
|---|---|---|---|---|
| **Future** | **Discover & Prove** | | **Execute & Repeat** | |
| Vision Statements | 10yr. Target / 3yr. Picture | | Cash/EBITDA/Profit | |
| Critical Success Factors Statements | 1yr. Plan / Goals / CSFs | | Measurables / Objectives | |
| Goals | Rocks | | Scorecards / Key Results | |
| Strategy Statements | Strategies | | Job & Role Purpose Statements | |
| Tactics | Tactics | | Process / Policy / Procedures / Work Instructions | |
| 1s | 2s | 3s | 4s | 5s |

SMART - STATE™ Model © WBCo (Specific Measurable Actionable Reviewable Time-bound Strategic Thinking and Tactical Execution)

The labels change, but most strategic planning has some version of these elements—the overall vision, the factors critical to its success, and then the goals, strategies, and tactics you'll use to make those factors a reality. We won't suggest which approach you should use here, but to maintain positive alignment on the critical need *to believe*, team members have to agree not only with the purpose but also with the organization's priorities and strategies for getting there. Someone who loves the destination but whines for the entire ride because he doesn't like the route is no fun to have in the car, right?

The purpose articulated in the organization's belief statement should be clearly connected to its strategic plan, which should be communicated on a regular basis to team members via your BOS thinking. They should be able to see how the plan aligns on an organizational level; a team level; and a WIIFM, individual level.

If after the strategy has been fully explained someone still can't align to your positive alignment, it's time to invite that budding entrepreneur to go and start his or her own organization.

Strategic planning is important, and we love it, but organizations run on people, not plans. The greatest plan in the world is useless if you have not surrounded yourself with people who belong, believe, are accountable, are measured well, are heard, developed, and balanced. A key impetus for the Seven Critical Needs came from my years of working with leaders on strategic plans and then watching them struggle to execute them. Without a deep well of courage and a way to constantly address those seven key areas, implementation is impossible.

 ## Diagnosing How Much Work You Need to Do as an Organization

### • TO BELIEVE •
*Exercise for PBOLTs and Senior Leadership to Answer*

Grab a piece of paper and follow these prompts.

1. Write down your organization's purpose, its *why*, in a belief statement.

2. Find three random members of the team—one senior leader, one midlevel person, and someone on the frontline—and ask: *What is the purpose of our organization?* Write down their answers.

3. When did you last use your *why*—the specific language noted in number 1 above—to arrive at a decision with team members or as a reference point in a meeting?

After completing the prompts below, review your answers—and don't fudge. Remember, you're the one with the answers. For each response, summarize how close to positive alignment your organization is on this critical need and give yourself a score from one of the following four choices:

**WAY FAR | MANY MILES | RIGHT AROUND THE CORNER | THERE**

## Scoring Guide

**How to Score Prompt 1:** *Write down your organization's purpose, its why, in a belief statement.*

- Was your answer more than a sentence? If so, you're either at Way Far or Many Miles.
- Could your statement be put in this form: *We believe in the power of* _____? If not, you're somewhere between Way Far and Right Around the Corner, not There.
- Could your statement be used to say no, to focus, to simplify? If not, you're Way Far.

**How to Score Prompt 2:** *Find three random members of the team—one senior leader, one midlevel person, and someone on the frontline—and ask: What is the purpose of our organization? Write down their answers.*

- Were their answers substantially similar? If not, you're Way Far.

**How to Score Prompt 3:** *When did you last use your why—the specific language noted in number 1 above—to arrive at a decision with team members or as a reference point in a meeting?*

- If your answer is more than two days out, you're somewhere between Way Far and Many Miles.

# CHAPTER 8

# To Be Accountable

---

**Critical Need 3. To Be Accountable**

**Organization Statement:** Our accountability and responsibility structure is clear; it is captured, communicated, and consistently updated.

**Team Member/Individual Statement:** I understand and embrace the purpose of my job and the roles that make up my job. I know what I should be thinking about and doing and why. **I am accountable.**

---

**JOB TITLES ARE** like giant blankets that obscure thought and action with their flat bulk. People who don't belong or believe often hide behind them, clinging like infants to those hollow labels for comfort and security.

Sure, we need legal titles to enter into contracts, but to describe a role or group of roles as chief this or vice that often muddies the waters rather than adding clarity.

Leaders, though, are reluctant to admit the inadequacies of titles. Many owners and leadership teams we work with recognize quickly that their organizations have not gotten to positive alignment on belonging and believing, but they think they're doing just fine in getting team members to understand and embrace what they are accountable for. "Look at this organizational chart," they say. "It's all right here. Alex, the marketing assistant, reports to Debbie, the marketing manager, who reports to Susan, the marketing director, who reports to Victor, the VP of marketing, who reports to Chuck, the COO, who reports to Sally, the CEO . . ."

Sorry, but that is not true accountability. Let's think about everything—we mean *everything*—that needs to be done in this organization, every quarter, month, week, day, minute, and second. Positive alignment on accountability means honestly assessing all the thinking and doing that must take place at an organization and then matching people with the inventory of thinking and doing roles that emerge from this exercise.

As we work on attaining positive alignment, we'll talk about the first positive alignments and a process, which is not easy or comfortable for team members. Here, we want to emphasize that "jobs" and "titles" are blunt instruments. Anyone who has worked at a big corporation knows that vice presidents can propagate like rabbits. Vice president of operations, vice president of sustainability, vice president of parking . . . What do these people *do*?

Thinking in terms of "role" clarifies the discussion. Each job contains many roles, and they shift over time. Some roles are purely about *thinking*. Some are purely *doing*. In my coaching and in these pages, we draw a distinction between "accountability" and "responsibility."

You are *accountable* for thinking—planning, considering, assessing a decision's potential impact. You are *responsible* for doing, for executing, for producing. Agreeing on these terms allows leaders and team members to clarify accountabilities and responsibilities. Do you understand and embrace both what you are accountable for thinking about and responsible for doing?

Many roles are a combination of thinking and doing, but organizations typically don't do the vital work of communicating how much time team members should be spending on each. Just considering the large number of roles at even small organizations, as well as how much thinking and doing is attached to each one, requires courage—doing the hard work your competition is unwilling to do. It is *so* much easier for them to be lazy, live in System 1 thinking, and hope that the titles on a direct report/org chart are good enough.

Recall the client we talked about earlier, Sine Tea, which brought us in as the company's expansion caused growing pains. Katrina, the vice president of culture and sustainability, had an impressive title and a well-paying job, but when we started talking about actual *roles*, no one could point to what a vice president of culture did. Sustainability was at the root of their *why*, and everyone was a part of that effort; sustainability was part of every role, so there was no need for a VP of that. Team members didn't know what Katrina was really supposed to be thinking about and doing.

Everyone assumed that Sine's chief financial officer performed the usual array of tasks people attach to that title, but when we drilled down into actual roles involving finance, it turned out that Bob, the owner, who had a strong financial background, loved the work and was filling many of the finance roles. He was good at these roles and frankly did not want to give them up. So, the clear answer was that the CFO could go, and a wonderful controller and financial reporting person could be hired to fill the roles that the CEO/owner did not want to fill. Sine had a typical org chart and the usual roster of titles, but these only distracted leadership from the overlap and gaps, as well as a number of org chart jobs that lacked purpose.

Titles are rarely descriptive enough, and forgive me for beating this drum again, but language matters. If we're not naming things accurately and consistently—a problem, a role, a core value—it is clear we don't believe in the same things. That makes clarity impossible and allows dysfunction. It endangers the shared belief and meaning that is the organization.

A one-and-done effort at defining roles doesn't solve all the problems either, since team members typically have to switch between them, depending on needs. At most organizations, roles change with particular seasons. At Layline.com, my sailboat racing gear dot-com, the nature of the business made those changes stark. Sales would start in mid-March and turn off in September or October, depending on the hurricane season. The shifts from heavy selling to heavy planning to heavy web and catalog execution meant that a team member's roles might switch from phone work to vendor relations to buying to copy-editing to photography.

Seasonal shifts in roles present challenges. Many humans, especially those engaged in System 1 lazy thinking, want to do the same thing every day. They seek familiarity and see it as a way to protect their certainty, autonomy, and other SCARF needs. Returning to my football analogy, I play center on offense and report to the offensive-line coach but must switch to the linebacker role and report to the defensive-back coach when it's time to play defense. Leaders and team members must coordinate constantly to ensure that roles are being filled in smart ways amid seasonal changes. Taking the time to do that difficult work requires constant vigilance and courage.

The process of attaining and maintaining positive alignment on accountabilities and responsibilities is a revelation for organizations.

Team members often are not aware of the roles they're currently filling until their organization insists on courageous analysis. We have all seen this at organizations we've been a part of. Someone jumps in to help out or pick up slack and, pretty soon, another task becomes part of their job. The job and title remain the same, but a role has been added.

A client we recently worked with shared that an employee was returning from maternity leave. The organization has 180 team members, and she was hired to work in her area of expertise, the benefits side of human resources, such as open enrollment and health plans. Her return was a perfect time to peel back the lid and look at roles. Before she left, she had been spending a lot of time on payroll, accounts payable, and accounts receivable, certainly not her highest and best use. We used this opportunity to realign, and the team loved it. At another organization, a salesperson was spending significant time thinking about development of a new product—a thinking role—when he really didn't have the authority for that role or the know-how or experience it required.

Clarifying roles helps all team members understand the purpose, domain, and authority of their "jobs"—a terrific model explained in the helpful book *Holacracy: The New Management System for a Rapidly Changing World*. Creating what a solid positive alignment looks like on this critical need of accountability is an involved process, but the benefits are enormous. The frustrations and confusion that come with "role creep"—the insidious, unconsidered, ad hoc accretion of tasks, duties, and expectations—tends to hurt the team members who belong and believe the most, the engaged. The engaged are the ones who jump in when someone's on leave, stay late when it's crunch time, pick up the ball someone else dropped. Over time, they can become uncertain about what they're really accountable for or can no longer embrace it. Their primary roles, the things they're best at and were hired for, might suffer as roles quietly morph. We are in the danger zone with these folks because the organization's BOS is not maintaining clear accountability.

Team members seek to answer positive alignment on this critical need because not understanding or embracing what they're accountable for is one of the biggest sources of frustration at organizations. This is where clarity disappears. Accountability ties back closely to SCARF—our primal need for status, certainty, autonomy, relatedness, and fairness. Those who belong and believe can't feel secure in terms of SCARF if they don't fully understand what they're accountable for. Hazy roles mean they have less certainty about what they will be thinking and doing in any given week. If they're taking over others' duties or being diverted from their own, relatedness and fairness suffer. Their sense of autonomy, a precondition for accountability, suffers. And all of this together can damage their status within the organization.

Accountability has to be addressed in conjunction with measurement.

## Attaining and Maintaining Positive Alignment on Accountability

One of the myths that nudged me into writing this book was the notion that millennials lack accountability. In my team's experience, there was no truth to this stereotype, so we began asking fresh team members what they wanted from work. Across the board, we found that millennials not only want accountability, but a lack of clear accountability at their organizations was a major source of frustration.

Too often, the millennials we interviewed said that, when talking about job accountabilities, leaders did not clearly outline or communicate what team members should be thinking about and doing. There was fuzziness about the *purpose* of their roles and how they connected to larger goals. They weren't always sure about who they reported to for which tasks or just how far their authority extended. Here yet again, it turned out, millennials wanted what we all want.

And we found that the team members who belonged and believed the most—they had the organization's core values and were behind its *why*—got the most upset about shaky accountability. These were the people who showed up eager to do a good job, and so they suffered the most frustration when shackled by poor accountability.

Apart from the obvious inefficiencies, this is one of the most damaging aspects of not aligning to positive alignment on critical need three—turning the A players into boxcars, destroying their courage. We discussed the neutrally engaged workers we call "boxcars" in part I—the people who show up and do the required work, stay off the brakes, but add no energy to the organization. We need boxcars—there are plenty out there, 22 percent—but we must be super diligent not to lose our engaged diamonds to negativity or neutrality.

## Promises Are a Two-Way Street

In his essay "Are There Any Natural Rights?" H. L. A. Hart paints the picture of a promise as a two-way street between the person making the promise and the person to whom the promise is made. By making a promise, a person confers certain rights to another person, which allows that person a degree of influence or authority over the person making the promise. It is the power to hold accountable. Hart writes:

> By promising to do or not to do something, we voluntarily incur obligations and create or confer rights on those to whom we promise; we alter the existing

moral independence of the parties' freedom of choice in relation to some action and create a new moral relationship between them, so that it becomes morally legitimate for the person to whom the promise is given to determine how the promisor shall act. That which corresponds very well to the distinction between a right, which an individual has, and what it is right to do. The promisee has a temporary authority or sovereignty in relation to some specific matter over the other's will which we express by saying that the promisor is under an obligation to the promisee to do what he has promised.

This two-way street formed by your Seven Promises will form the bedrock of your culture.

It is this promise that empowers everyone in your organization to hold you accountable, and that accountability will make you a better leader. Of course, that accountability flows both ways as your team members agree to be held accountable to the company's core values, mission, and standards when they take the job. Mutual accountability to clear standards is the surest path to trust and great results.

Setting up a clear accountability structure replaces that frustration with courage. In conjunction with positive alignment on the rest of the Seven Critical Needs, it allows you to build engagement among top team members and unleashes a powerful force. Maintaining positive alignment on this critical need is a key way of addressing SCARF needs. Clear accountability is absolutely necessary for status, certainty, autonomy, relatedness, and fairness.

Positive alignment on accountability takes serious work—no, your current direct report or org chart alone won't cut it—but once you've done the work, you save enormous time and energy because you can lead rather than merely manage. People who are clear about their roles, their purpose, and what they need to be thinking and doing every day feel liberated. They have a greater sense of direction. It sounds counterintuitive perhaps, but accountability actually brings freedom. Team members answering positive alignment on accountability can work with certainty and autonomy. They know their zone and are comfortable in it.

Positive alignment on accountability improves team cohesion and performance too. The painstaking work of delineating all roles and making sure that every task, idea, and issue is captured eliminates tensions, insecurities, and petty squabbles. Team members now know how they relate to everyone else at the organization. They're aware of their own and each other's status, and the fairness quotient rises. Tim, who resented being drafted to help with payroll every Thursday, is no longer annoyed, either because a course correction moves him out of that ad hoc role or because it becomes his, officially. If this needs to be one of his roles, leadership explains how much space it should take up, the thinking and doing requirements, and how it relates to the organization's *why*.

Our example might seem like a distinction without a difference—Tim is doing the exact same work, but *owning* the role, with real accountability, can be the difference between a star and a boxcar. People in various roles need to own the processes and procedures that define their work and be partly accountable for developing and refining them. This is why the responsibility of positive alignment here begins to shift to the team member, with about 65 percent of the weight shouldered by the organization and the remaining 35 percent by the individual.

Leadership must start the process, though, by pressing an initiative that takes an inventory of everything that needs to be done and every role and position, setting aside for the moment jobs and titles.

The role of your BOS is to be sure this is not a one-time exercise. Roles should be assessed all the time, at a minimum every season. Do team members understand the amount of thinking versus doing that they should be engaged in for each role? Do they understand the boundaries of their domain and how much authority they have? Are they clear on the purpose of each role and how it relates to the overall *why*?

This is the reality that Bryan Bunker, the COO of Nöel Group, shared.

"The workplace is complicated," Bunker says. "When you start getting into organizations of a certain size, that complexity multiplies, and it's not a linear complexity, it's exponential. If you don't have your arms around that, things can break down in so many different ways, especially when it comes time to pivot."

The classic org chart does not wrap your arms around or allow you to see the complexity; the tools of your BOS must.

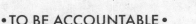

## Diagnosing How Much Work You Need to Do as an Organization

### • TO BE ACCOUNTABLE •

*Exercise for PBOLTs and Senior Leadership to Answer*

Grab a piece of paper and follow these prompts.

1. Have you inventoried everything that needs to be thought about and done at the organization and defined which employees are filling which roles (not just "jobs")? Yes or no?

2. When was the last time you discussed with a team member the amount of thinking versus doing he or she should engage in for a particular role?

3. Do all "titles" at the organization accurately reflect the roles within their domain?

4. When was the last time something important did not get done because team members were not sure who was responsible for it?

After completing the prompts above, review your answers using my highly unscientific key below—and don't fudge. Remember, you're the one with the answers, and you probably know in your gut, without reading another word, how far you are from positive alignment. For each of your answers, give yourself a score from one of the following four choices:

**WAY FAR | MANY MILES | RIGHT AROUND THE CORNER | THERE**

## Scoring Guide

**How to Score Prompt 1:** *Have you inventoried everything that needs to be thought about and done at the organization and defined which employees are filling which roles (not just "jobs")? Yes or no?*

- If you answered no, you're Way Far. If yes, you're somewhere between Right Around the Corner and There.

**How to Score Prompt 2:** *When was the last time you discussed with a team member the amount of thinking versus doing he or she should engage in for a particular role?*

- If the answer is more than a week or two, you're Many Miles away. More than that and you're Way Far.

**How to Score Prompt 3:** *Do all "titles" at the organization accurately reflect the roles within their domain?*

- If you answered no, you're not alone, but you are somewhere between Way Far and Right Around the Corner.

**How to Score Prompt 4:** *When was the last time something important did not get done because team members were not sure who was responsible for it?*

- If the answer is less than a month, you're somewhere between Way Far and Right Around the Corner, but you probably are not There.
- If it was yesterday and the day before, you're likely Way Far.

# CHAPTER 9

# To Be Measured

**PATRICK LENCIONI, IN** his book *Three Signs of a Miserable Job*, which morphed into *The Truth About Employee Engagement*, points out the three signs of a terrible job: (1) being irrelevant, (2) being anonymous, and (3) being unmeasured. He argues that these are three of the largest factors that lead to disengagement. Gino Wickman argues hard in his book *Traction* that reporting to a weekly scorecard is not a trap but a freeing event. We say give a person a solid measure, so they know if they are doing a good job, and they can go home at the end of the week and feel good about themselves. This translates to the entire world when we eliminate worry.

Wickman argues that everyone in the organization should have at least one number that they know they own.

All the Seven Critical Needs are tightly interconnected, but perhaps none more so than critical needs three and four. An organization must define its jobs and roles and make sure team members understand what they are accountable for and responsible for before it can measure performance, and without good ways to measure performance, there is no true accountability.

As I hope you appreciate by now, each "job" might include five, six, seven roles, which may change according to the seasons of a particular industry. Organizations typically have broad measures of overall performance in place, but each of a team member's roles should have some sort of deliverable, a particular measure for that particular role. The same set of metrics won't work for all team members, obviously. What constitutes a good job for a salesperson, a truck driver, and an accountant varies widely. Leaders get this, but they often fail to recognize that metrics should be attached to each role within a job. Metrics paint the picture and allow employees to be accountable for their defined roles.

I always tried to teach and coach so my folks could visualize what the numbers were *saying*. At Layline, we oriented around margins: margin in dollars, as a percent of gross, as net, as gross-margin return on investment, all sorts of good numbers that we wanted people to understand so we could have robust conversations and make rational decisions. These numbers were the bottom-line language of Layline as an organization. A great resource is Alex Freytag's book *Profit Works*. He cowrote it with Tom Bouwer—we hand it to all our clients when they utter the phrase "incentive plans," and we say, "Oh, you are talking about 'we-Comp'"—a term coined by Alex. We-comp versus me-comp—how we all benefit from hitting our profit numbers. All for one, one for all stuff = powerful.

We were a catalogue retailer and a dot-com, and we sold at shows and events—and each of these venues was a statistics honey hole. We worked with SAS (statistical analysis systems), the largest privately held software company on the planet, in the early days. My next-door neighbor was a VP there, and we were using the same beta software as NationsBank to analyze our customer behavior and predict future behavior. This wasn't backroom stuff. We brought it out to our front-line folks to help them understand why we were making decisions and how they could impact the results of our experiments. The numbers spoke to us and helped us speak.

Positive measures should build your team members' confidence in the decisions they make and the results they can achieve. This sort of measurement is a lot like setting up your sailboat to go scorchingly fast in the upcoming race. We can't see the wind, but we can see the things that impact our decisions. We can see, for instance, that the waves are just starting to form whitecaps, which means the wind is blowing between eight and ten knots. We can look at our compass and see the direction it's blowing and which way our boat will head. We can look at the clouds and make a prediction about where the wind, waves, and currents are headed. Using that data set, we can compare it to our "tune sheet," to choose if we'll use light-air, heavy-air, or medium-air equipment. That data tells us how tight to set the rig and the sails to go fast.

Just as we cannot see the wind when sailing, we can't see the future or into the minds of our customers in business either. We must collect and use data to make predictions. With awareness of this data, we can look to our tune sheet, or our setup sheet, to be sure we are set up to achieve our ultimate goal.

A good measure set allows our people to see, discuss, and ultimately drive courageous, repeatable results. A bad set can focus on long-term measurement at the expense of short-term metrics, or vice versa. A strong business operating system will ensure that good measurement has both long-term and short-term components. Whether the standard metrics are sales quotas, number of customers retained, or number of workers recruited, leaders must clearly communicate the endgame. *Here is our why. Here is what success looks like long term and how your roles align with our overall purpose.* MBAs call these long-term measures "lagging indicators."

Leading indicators, much like their macroeconomic counterparts, measure activity along the way, as we move toward that endgame. Team members should think: *Here are the things I can work on, every day and every week, in pursuit of that larger goal. Here are the numbers that will let me know how well I'm progressing.* Too often, leaders don't establish clear leading indicators with team members, or worse, never have regular conversations around them.

Note that we said leaders should establish metrics "with team members." When team members resist being measured and feel locked down or hampered by the process, that's often because it didn't include them. They might consider the metrics unfair or inaccurate. Giving them a voice in how they're measured can lead to creative and more accurate ways to track progress. Such conversations also give leaders a chance to explain why certain numbers are important to them and how the team members' roles relate to the overall goal. The metric that seemed unfair might get buy-in once leaders courageously explain their point of view. Having the conversation is key. Organizations that can't attain and maintain positive alignment on the critical need *to be measured* inevitably fall short on the next critical need: *to be heard*.

Establishing metrics with team members builds a powerful sense of belonging and belief—the two foundations of the Seven Critical Needs. Someone who is brought into the process no longer sees the agreed-on measurement as a leash or a limitation but a means to autonomy. What sort of thinking and doing is necessary to hit these near and far targets?

We are not arguing for low standards or a free-for-all. The metrics must be agreed to by leaders and team members, and they must make sense for each role as well as the organization as a whole. But unless team members have a voice in how they're measured, they can't have real autonomy. Without autonomy, leaders can't lead—only manage. And management without leadership, as we've pointed out, is difficult, time-consuming, and stunting for the organization.

"Autonomy" is at the heart of SCARF, and getting to positive alignment on measurement is vital to meeting SCARF needs. Good metrics provide certainty and fairness because team members know and have agreed on how they are measured. It's hard to say that something you helped make and agreed to is unclear or unfair. On the other hand, if the rules are always changing midgame in a free-for-all, the primal threat response will kick in and System 1 irrational thinking will take over.

Objective, open metrics feed into team members' feelings of relatedness and status too. People in similar roles are measured by similar numbers. They see how others are doing and exactly where they fit in the tribe. If they are doing a good job, their status is probably secure.

The process we are describing takes—you guessed it—courage. Dropping a quota on someone from on high does not require collaboration, conversations, adjustments, or frankly, much thinking. Neither do standard KPIs—the key performance indicators found in every industry. While many might be useful, we are generally not a fan of just accepting this type of measurement, because it's generic and not particular to the organization. If you are a lazy System 1 thinker, sure, go with the industry standard, the way everyone measures things—take it away. If you are a courageous System 2 thinker, you will challenge the crap and come up with something your organization really believes.

A client that has more than 60 Great Clips hair salons is a good example of what we mean here. Their measure was the one espoused by the franchise: customer count. How many people are we getting in the door? Lately, they realized that the real riddle is haircutter retention. The organization's purpose is "joy through growth," and to fulfill it, they discovered, they must focus heavily on retaining haircutters, an important driver of customer count. They now have a haircutter retention role with long-term and short-term metrics in place to achieve that goal. Retain great haircutters = job number one!

Performing the difficult work of creating such custom, collaborative metrics requires courage, but it builds courage as well. It creates the focus and boundaries courage demands. Team members can prioritize, and they learn to appreciate how even the most menial or painful short-term work is fulfilling a long-term purpose. They aren't wigging out on a regular basis, treating all work as equal, or focusing on the wrong stuff. Good measurement, you might say, is a kind of vaccine against "busy fool syndrome."

## Attaining and Maintaining Positive Alignment on Being Measured

Perhaps the biggest problem with measuring is that organizations approach it as something done *to* team members. Performance evaluations, one of the most common forms of measurement that has carried forward from the Dark Ages, are generally top down and tinged with a passive, punitive aura. Even team members who consistently get "exceeds expectations" and rave reviews grow nervous at review time because they have as much control over and participation in the process as a film director waiting to see if her premier got panned.

I remember my four years at EY, a "big eight" CPA firm. We would come to the end of the year, and some dude who has not even talked to you in the last six months is rating you on a rating scale/rubric you have never seen. They just pop it on you once a year with no communication during the year.

The courageously patient organization wants team members to positively align with the critical need, to understand *and embrace* the ways they are measured. We have highlighted "embrace" because that's the key piece of this puzzle that organizations almost universally neglect. If measurement is treated like a leash or a stick or a pat on the head, positive alignment here becomes impossible.

We need to view the whole idea of measurement in new terms in order to engage employees and build courage. Note that of the Seven Critical Needs, this one is the pivot, the point at which the organization does half the work of positive alignment and the individual does the other half. Typical measures such as the performance review place 90 to 100 percent of the burden on the organization while the team member sits passively and, well, takes it.

Patrick Lencioni, in his book *Three Signs of a Miserable Job*, points to three areas: anonymous, irrelevant, and unmeasured. AIM is the acronym I use.

Measurement is something we are doing for and with our people; it is how we honor them and trust them; it is how we create clarity around status, certainty, autonomy, relatedness, and fairness. When they are able to deliver the agreed-upon measurables, they feel comfortable about their status and relatedness—we are a hunter and gatherer tribe; I delivered my three pounds of nuts this week. I understand the tribe is going in this direction, and I delivered the values that support this direction adding certainty. I embrace my measures and was able to use some creative strategies to deliver my measures this week, giving room for autonomy. Avoiding surprises with clear measures is the agreement backbone around what job accountabilities are all about—with clear agreement around how someone is measured, we create the baseline for fairness.

 ## Diagnosing How Much Work You Need to Do as an Organization

### •TO BE MEASURED •
*Exercise for PBOLTs and Senior Leadership to Answer*

Grab a piece of paper and follow these prompts.

1. Do all roles—not just jobs—have objective measures built in?
2. Do those measures include obtainable numbers and both short-term and long-term components?
3. How often are senior leaders meeting with team members to get their input on and discuss metrics?
4. When is the last time you highlighted for team members the ways that their metrics connect to the organization's *why*?

After completing the prompts below, review your answers using the key, below—and don't fudge. Remember, you're the one with the answers, and you probably know in your gut, without reading another word, how far you are from positive alignment. Summarize how close to positive alignment your organization is on this critical need by scoring your responses. For each answer, give yourself a score from one of these four choices:

**WAY FAR | MANY MILES | RIGHT AROUND THE CORNER | THERE**

## Scoring Guide

**How to Score Prompt 1:** *Do all roles—not just jobs—have objective measures built in?*

- If you answered no, you're Way Far. If yes, you might be somewhere between Right Around the Corner and There.

**How to Score Prompt 2:** *Do those measures include obtainable numbers and both short-term and long-term components?*

- If you answered no, you're Way Far. If yes, you're somewhere between Right Around the Corner and There.

**How to Score Prompt 3:** *How often are senior leaders meeting with team members to get their input on and discuss metrics?*

- If your answer was more than 90 days, you're Many Miles or Way Far. If it's 90 days or less, you might just be There.

**How to Score Prompt 4:** *When is the last time you highlighted for team members the ways that their metrics connect to the organization's why?*

- If your answer was more than 90 days, you're Way Far. If it's 90 days or less, you might just be There.

# CHAPTER 10

## To Be Heard

---

**Critical Need 5. To Be Heard**

**Organization Statement:** We have clear, consistent communication mechanisms and channels in place. They promote listening and responding, build trust, spur debate, solve problems, and allow individuals to participate in being heard.

**Team Member/Individual Statement:** I understand and embrace how and when my organization listens and responds. **I am heard.**

---

EVEN EFFICIENT, FUNCTIONAL organizations with a clear purpose and strong core values tend to have meetings that live somewhere between poor and *please shoot me*. Meetings aren't the only way that opinions get heard in an organization, but they provide one of the most egregious examples of how leaders fall down when it comes to hearing team members.

As Patrick Lencioni argues, "Reasonable human beings do not need to get their way in order to support a decision, but only need to know that their opinions have been heard and considered."

Leaders with the courage to structure and use meetings effectively can create meetings that people not only find useful but actually look forward to attending. Yes, we are serious. Meetings tend to be handled so poorly, people can begin to think the terrain is naturally half swamp. We completely disagree, but more on meetings later. First, we want to explore why it is so important that team members understand and embrace how they are heard. We all want to be heard, and when we're not—whether it's at work, in a marriage, or as part of a club—we check out.

Communication, as I presented in part I, is our unique gift as humans. It is our greatest example of a leap forward in intersubjectivity, the ability to share meaning. If leaders communicate their expectations, goals, and feedback but don't have good mechanisms in place for listening, team members grow frustrated and impatient. All failures of listening are, at root, failures of courage. Building clear channels of communication that allow team members to be heard, challenge the status quo, express fears, voice options, spur debate, admit mistakes, and ultimately drive to agreement is a vital part of becoming a courageously patient organization.

Many organizations never establish a solid rhythm for their meeting structure. Meetings are ad hoc, vague, or drifting. Team members want to know: *Okay, now is the time when we talk about X. This is the time to plan strategy for Y or give feedback on Z.* This builds their feelings of certainty and relatedness because they know what's coming, who will be involved, how their time will be invested, and how it aligns with the larger purpose.

For millions of years the seasons ruled our lives, and that rhythm remains engrained in us. Perhaps growing up involved in a family farm has made me especially aware of the pattern, but as someone who has run four very seasonal companies and coached leadership teams at hundreds of others, I can tell you that there is something magical about the 90-day mark we keep returning to. Whether we bring this up at a nonprofit or a major corporation, when we point it out, leaders tend to agree that things need a kind of reset every three months. We think this is due to the natural changing of the seasons.

We believe a strong BOS ensures that every individual at an organization will be communicated with, heard, confirmed, and aligned at least every 90 days, or once a season. Similarly, we will ask if your BOS is guiding a meeting inventory to test the utility, labeling, and attendance of every single meeting at the organization every 90 days.

Here, we want to point out that many of the roadblocks to getting to and maintaining positive alignment on the critical need *to be heard* stem from language. As I said, *it's all semantics.* Language matters. Too many leaders carefully plan a meeting but don't have the courage to name it with care and accuracy. What you call the meeting conveys among other things the type of communication channel it will provide for team members and how they can expect to listen and to be heard in it.

This is the same principle we argued for in our discussions of core values and an organization's *why.* You can't enjoy positive alignment without getting the language right. Whether you're naming core values or a weekly meeting, lazy, loose, or conflicting language means people don't believe the same thing, and as we've pointed out, your organization is nothing more than the belief of its members. Getting the language wrong isn't a mere oversight but an existential threat, and leaders can't build a courageous organization without understanding this.

As leaders build courage and make progress toward positive alignment on the Seven Critical Needs, they create context for all communication. Making team members feel that they are heard is not as simple as 10 minutes to bend a supervisor's ear each week. If they are getting to and maintaining positive alignment on belonging, believing, accountability, and measurement, team members will share with leaders a common language and a sense of the big picture. *Why are we having this conversation?* Those who belong and believe understand how their feedback fits into the organization's purpose and strengthens core values alignment.

Listening is a vital way for the courageously patient organization to leverage strengths and overcome weaknesses, to exploit opportunities and avoid threats. Picture a topographic map or navigational chart where hazards, channels, markers, and weather forecasts are all out in the open. The only way to ensure that the best ideas are noted, biggest opportunities are identified, and worst problems are solved is to insist that all voices are heard.

Understanding and embracing the way that team members are heard builds deep reservoirs of trust in them—the foundation of a model I called EATT. You'll recall this stands for evolve, adapt, trust, try, and it's the prerequisite for any organization to be a living, growing thing, as opposed to a soulless machine. Team members who are heard in positive ways have enough trust to voice dissent, take risks, and admit mistakes, to evolve and adapt. They are free to engage in the fearless System 2 thinking that drives competitive advantage.

## Attaining and Maintaining Positive Alignment on Being Heard

If you don't feel that you're being heard, why toss out a fresh idea? Why point out inefficiencies that could be corrected or suggest a new process? Why mention the things that would make you more engaged or productive at work? Why say anything at all unless it's in response to direct questions?

People need to feel that they're being heard in order to get anywhere, which is why getting team members to align with understanding and embracing how they are heard is vital. Not being heard, whether it's because people don't have the courage to listen or because the channels of communication are inadequate, not only hurts the individual's engagement, but it also stymies the organization by smothering innovation, stifling feedback, and crippling collaboration.

For team members to feel that they're being heard, leaders must learn to actively listen. Obvious, right? We agree, but that does not make the act of listening any easier inside an organization with as many personality types as there are team members, as many problems to solve as there are hours in the day, as many deadlines as there are days. Listening in the midst of what the 4DX business operating system calls "the whirlwind"—the daily exigencies of work—requires time and effort. Perhaps most of all, it requires courage. It is the job of your BOS to install and maintain the organization's methods for hearing.

When I ask people what the word "courage" brings to mind, some version of *listening, hearing, or good listener* tops the list. You cannot become a courageously patient organization without listening to your members—all of them. And getting them to embrace the ways they are heard and how and when the organization listens are the job of your BOS.

Each of the Seven Critical Needs requires that people are *heard*. If you need certain skills to *belong*, will someone listen as you explain the deficit and help you acquire those skills? Nodding with a sympathetic smile is not *hearing* if you immediately forget what was just said or do nothing about it. If you don't understand how parts of an announced strategy align with the organization's *why*, is there a channel that allows you to express that concern? Is your feedback on rubrics *heard* in ways that help you buy into and say yes on *measurement*? As we'll soon explore, the last two of the Seven Critical Needs, on development and balance, require individuals to do the heavy lifting, but that's impossible if they are speaking in a vacuum. Sound does not travel in the vacuum of outer space. For sound to travel, your BOS must lay down how the organization listens.

This critical need about being heard is the first of the seven where most of the work falls on the individual, around 70 percent. The organization, however, must address its 30 percent of the effort before the individual can work on his or her share. Clear channels, mechanisms, and strategies that allow for true hearing must be established. For people to be heard, the channels have to be two way, not simply top down. This also sounds obvious, we realize, and yet every organization we've encountered needs work in this area.

As Lencioni argues, the basis for embracing the effort it takes to be heard is trust, and the way to build trust is by maintaining positive alignment to the Seven Critical Needs. Language, we have argued, is what allows humans to come together in groups to solve complex problems. The conference call, email thread, and Skype session are modern versions of tribal elders passing the talking stick around the fire outside the cave. We are social animals that over eons evolved with language. It's embedded in our brains, but the technological progress that has moved us forward has also been a step back in some ways.

Text-based electronic communication is necessary and efficient, but it removes a layer of perception that evolved over millions of years to help humans survive. Communicating through a device is a little like having a conversation in noise-cancelling headphones while listening to your favorite book in the background. You'll hear most words, but you've dulled a few key senses. Have you ever attempted a joke on email that fell flat, was taken as serious, or worse, offended someone, though your intentions were innocent? The exact same words uttered face-to-face are much less likely to be misread, partly because tone and expression of voice and body language tell us so much. The static zeros and ones that make it to our screens are miraculous but not equal for the nuance of a human voice, which we react to biologically in endless, important ways.

Phone calls, of course, involve a clear human voice. They must be just as good as meeting in person, right? Not really. Much like tone of voice, facial expressions and body language convey immense amounts of data. Research has shown that much, perhaps most, information processing occurs in the brain with no accompanying conscious experience. Some of the processing becomes conscious later, but much of it influences perception and behavior without our awareness.

Many of our judgments based on facial expressions and features—even those glimpsed in milliseconds—prove surprisingly accurate. Research has shown that this includes things that would seem impossible to predict, including how much money a CEO will make for the company in a given year and the leadership skills of executives as measured in bottom-line profits. Most of us understand that we have a better sense of skepticism or enthusiasm or slight hesitancy when we see a face reacting, or a head nod, but that's only the tip of the iceberg. Our brains are processing massive amounts of data and important nuances every minute that we're with another human.

Our advice when it comes to upping effective communication is to *go verbal—you know, use your vocal cords, your voice—*whenever possible. By this we don't mean just a phone call but real voices emanating from real bodies in the same room. There is no substitute for this kind of human interaction when it comes to being fully heard and listening actively. Of course, email, texting, calls, and videoconferences have their uses, but how often these days are we trading emails with someone down the hall when a quick face-to-face would actually take less time? Such interactions are richer, and through them, our primal SCARF needs are more likely to be met. We think most of us would agree that our feelings of status, certainty, and relatedness in particular are richer when we're looking someone in the eye.

Meetings are the most common way of *going verbal* in organizations. The most important meeting for positive alignment on being heard, and on all of the Seven Critical Needs, is the 7Q Yeses Seasonal Meeting. We will examine this further in the chapter on *being developed*. This one-on-one reset is a chance for a team member to go over rubrics with their coach and to see how well they as an individual are aligned with core values and the organization's *why*. It is also a chance to listen as the team member assesses whether he or she is at positive alignment on the Seven Critical Needs.

Meetings are an indispensable extension of our tribal roots, but they also provide ample evidence that going verbal is no guarantee people will be heard. Meetings start or run late. They have the wrong names, weak agendas, unclear objectives, poor focus, or the wrong attendees—all items your BOS should handle and address.

An important part of positive alignment to being heard involves finding the right rhythm for your meetings. That process starts with deciding on the type of meeting you're scheduling and is the bailiwick of your BOS. Earlier, we discussed the two main categories as defined by Michael Gerber, author of *The E-Myth*. He distinguishes between "in" meetings, which discuss daily work, tasks, and problems, and "on" meetings, which rise above daily and monthly concerns to focus on systemic issues, long-term goals, and the future of the business. Deciding whether meetings are *in* or *on* is a great way to begin focusing on them. If it's an *in* meeting, don't drift off into a discussion of the three-year plan—the immediate problems won't get solved. Likewise, don't let the *on* meeting get hijacked by this week's sluggish sales. Again, this is the job of your BOS to challenge your Meeting Pulse (EOS), Meeting Rhythm (Habits), Meeting Stew (the Advantage), or Meetings (the fourth discipline of execution in 4DX).

It's also helpful, after you consider Gerber's broad classification, to get more specific. Is this an informational meeting, called solely to convey data, news, or procedures? If so, the 80-20 rule might be in effect: the leader or facilitator will speak around 80 percent of the time, and the remaining 20 percent will be Q&A. If it's a brainstorming meeting, the format might be looser, with speaking time divided fairly evenly around the room. Your BOS should be the guide to making decisions around your types and timing.

## Get Your Hearing Tested

So how *verbal* is your team?

Find out. Choose a date and call it "communication day"—a typical Tuesday or Wednesday will do. Have everyone at the organization log every interaction during the workday, noting how long it lasted and the medium, such as in-person conversation, phone, email. Ask people to calculate the percentage of time they spent on each form of communication and then tally the organization-wide totals to share with all team members. What can you learn from the results? Are there any correlations between those who seem most successful or productive and the percentage of time they spend communicating in a particular way? Are there any connections between those who seem to have communication issues and their reliance on a particular medium?

To take it further, tell staff that during the next month, you would like them—within reason and without interrupting workflow—to communicate in person whenever possible. Release the Velcro holding you to your seat and pop over to talk to Tim in accounting to discuss a client who stopped paying invoices rather than trading four emails.

Visit HR with your benefits questions rather than dialing the extension. Near the end of the month, take another tally. How much, if at all, has the percentage of face-to-face conversation risen? Solicit feedback from team members. What did they think of the experiment? How, if at all, did it affect their work quality, productivity, sense of belonging and believing? Have leaders noticed any marked improvements or drop-offs as a result of the change?

 ## Diagnosing How Much Work You Need to Do as an Organization

### •TO BE HEARD•
*Exercise for PBOLTs and Senior Leadership to Answer*

Grab a piece of paper and follow these prompts.

1. What percentage of your time is spent listening to team members?
2. On a scale of 1–10, how would attendees rate meeting effectiveness on average at your organization?
3. When is the last time you took a meeting inventory, assessing the utility, name, or attendance of every meeting at the organization?

After completing the prompts above, review your answers using my key below. Summarize how close to positive alignment your organization is on this critical need—and don't fudge. Remember, you're the one with the answers, and you probably know in your gut, without reading another word, how far you are from positive alignment. For each of your responses, give yourself a score from one of these four choices:

**WAY FAR | MANY MILES | RIGHT AROUND THE CORNER | THERE**

## Scoring Guide

**How to Score Prompt 1:** *What percentage of your time is spent listening to team members?*

- If it's less than 10 percent, you're Way Far from positive alignment, less than 20 percent you're Many Miles away. If it's 30 percent or more, you're Right Around the Corner or There.

**How to Score Prompt 2:** *On a scale of 1–10, how would attendees rate meeting effectiveness on average at your organization?*

- If you can't answer because you don't ask attendees to rate meetings, you're Way Far. If the answer was lower than 7, you're Way Far.
- If you can honestly answer 7 or above, you're Right Around the Corner or There.

**How to Score Prompt 3:** *When is the last time you took a meeting inventory, assessing the utility, name, or attendance of every meeting at the organization?*

- If the answer is more than 90 days, you're somewhere between Many Miles and Way Far.

# CHAPTER 11

# To Be Developed

---

### Critical Need 6. To Be Developed

**Organization Statement:** We have consistent, repeatable mechanisms in place that help team members take charge of their own development.

**Team Member/Individual Statement:** I understand and embrace my organization's development mechanisms and how I can develop; I know how to take an active role in my own development. **I am developed.**

---

**DEVELOPMENT OF TEAM** members is critical not just when it comes to sharpening skills and building competitive advantage, it is yet another place where the Seven Critical Needs allow you to combat the depressingly low engagement numbers we have quoted from Gallup. True development allows team members to tune into WIIFM and to connect their personal *why* to the organization's *why*.

Team members who understand and appreciate opportunities for development have greater motivation, trust, and loyalty. Attaining and maintaining positive alignment to this critical need keeps them belonging and believing, although the relationship is circular: *maintaining positive alignment on the previous five critical needs should also provide an organic path to positive alignment on this one.*

Leaders often underestimate the power of development because they take a narrow, impatient view of it. We say "development," and they think training, certifications, a safety course, a conference, continuing education. All of those are fine and have their place, but positive alignment to this critical need requires a broader, more courageous perspective of development.

The things we just mentioned tend to come from on high. They are predicated on a one-way top-down approach to development. True development is both more complex and simpler than that.

Development is more complex in the context of the Seven Critical Needs because it's one of the main planks in building a courageously patient organization and not just a box to check. How does this team member's growth align with the organization's growth? How does his or her development align with the organization's core values and its *why*? How can individual needs be met and skills boosted in ways that allow a team member to get to positive alignment on belonging?

*A structure for development will emerge organically with the seven.*

Of course, development can include a Microsoft certification or equipment training, but it might also mean a weekly conversation with a leader. It could mean work on changing a particular habit, eliminating a regular duty to make time for thinking, or a teaching assignment. Strategic shuffling, rotations, cross-training of the roles that are part of a given job in ways that make sense for both the organization and the individual can fall under the development umbrella too.

That's the complicated part.

In a way, though, the process we are describing is simpler than the usual top-down view, too, because, if your BOS is ensuring that you are maintaining a positive alignment answer to the previous five critical needs, *a path for development should emerge organically.* If the team member can say, "Yes, I believe in the core values and the *why* that the organization has clearly presented, I understand my roles, what I am accountable for, and how my work is measured," then he or she should be able to say, "I need to work on X and Y. Here are the skills I must learn or sharpen to contribute to WIIFM and my organization."

The Seven Critical Needs are tightly interwoven, and in a very real sense, team members begin working on critical need six—*Am I Developed?*—the day that they and the organization start working on critical need one: *to belong.* Part of belonging, remember, is being able to say, *Yes, I have or can develop the skill sets needed for my roles.*

This more organic and holistic view of development puts the team member in charge. Development can't be done *to* or *for* someone. The organization should be *with* team members as they embrace their own development.

My coach, Greg Walker, uses the phrase "two lives working on one"—rather than "mentoring"—precisely because we don't like the top-down relationship this development term implies. This kind of mutually beneficial relationship and the broader view of development we are advocating require courage. It's much easier to think about a standard training regimen, but helping team members take control of their own development sews courage into the fabric of the organization too. It builds trust and loyalty and encourages them to take the long view of a personal *why* that's intertwined with the organizational *why.* Just as leaders must have the courage to work *on* a business, they must also have the courage to allow individuals who want to progress to work *on* themselves.

All of this might sound like it requires large amounts of additional work. The journey requires courage, as we said, but in the aggregate, it actually takes less work. As team members progress on their own development, they create templates for their roles and for individuals throughout the organization. Positive alignment to this and the other critical needs over time provides useful, organic, employee-created collaterals, including process, procedure, maintenance, training, and development materials that can be used in the future, saving leaders and the courageously patient organization tons of time. A good BOS helps you repeat and capture this effort too.

## Attaining and Maintaining Positive Alignment on Development

Most team members want to develop, and if a path for their development isn't clear, the organization is likely to lose them. Development might involve a class, a certification, a conference, or safety training, but it also could include changing a habit, meeting regularly with a coach, or taking on a new role.

These, however, are tactics. Such efforts need to exist in support of clear strategies that help realize long-term, future-based development goals. People want development, but often, not the hard work it requires, just as many of us want to get fit but find reasons to avoid the gym. It's easy to rationalize putting off certification on a new machine or the time commitment of an evening class when you have a busy workday. Development requires courage, and the organization can cultivate it by helping team members turn their attention to their futures.

The organization's active role here is relatively small—perhaps 20 percent of the effort—but important and should be mapped by your BOS. The other 80 percent of the effort is truly up to the individual whose effort will be directly influenced by three factors.

## Three Development Influencers

Three areas influence one's commitment to their own development—again a triangulation: the organization or tribe, the team or family, and the individual or self.

Tribally, one's development will be influenced by the idea of swimming with the current or against the current. The job of the BOS for the organization is to clearly set and communicate this direction so the individual can understand if he or she is motivated, neutral, or demotivated by it; simple but super important. Going to work and swimming against the current of where you imagine your future is exhausting and cannot be maintained. The tribe is migrating, and it is going to be cold and hard. Do you want to come along? Yes or no?

One's work family/team/squad has more impact on development than we often acknowledge; this is where the on-the-job training happens. EATT applies again. Organizations and people, in order to survive, must evolve; in order to evolve, they must adapt; in order to adapt, they must trust. Then they must try—that is, figure out what and why something works. Evolve, adapt, trust, try. The role of a family/team in the development of the individual is to create the events as part of the natural flow of work. Teams are the best at seeing what is working and what is not working. They are best at determining what we will try next. In other words, teammates are given opportunities to EATT. It is not something truly planned for the individual; it just happens as the normal part of teamwork.

Your BOS plays a part in this on-the-job development. In the world of EOS and Rockefeller Habits, they use short-term "Rocks," while 4DX extracts short-term goals out of what they call "the whirlwind" via a team meeting known as the WIG Session. Rocks and 4DX goals are owned by individuals and are typically things a bit outside of the normal day—driving *trying* that drives *adaptation* that helps the organization and individual evolve. The team leader is the one accountable for driving the EATT pattern. Get this type of rotation moving in your organization, and the waterwheel will turn from the weight of your individuals developing.

## Promises Infer Rights

David Owens proposes a power based on what he calls our "authority interest," the power that being the recipient of a promise gives us: "If you promise me a lift home, *this promise gives me the right* to require you to drive me home; in that sense, it puts me in authority over you."

Our Seven Promises are going to be inferring rights on our people, where we are establishing the expectation that we are going to keep our promises. If we allow people to hang around who do not belong, who do not demonstrate our core values, then we'd better get ready to have our people call us out or maybe even leave because they now see leadership as liars.

A team leader must be AAAA: aligned, accountable, authentic, and aware. In order to lead, each team member must see their leader as aligned to the overall good, accountable in doing what you say you are doing to do, authentic in that you are honest about yourself, and aware. These four words are a mash-up of the work of Dr. Stephen

Covey's *Speed of Trust* and Dr. John Grinnell's *Beyond Belief.* If you are faking it in any of the four *A*s, your folks will smell it and will not commit to follow.

The third influencer is one's imagined future self. Humans are motivated by the future and just need help going into that future and mapping a path back to the present. Some folks are natural future people. "Futuristic" is one of Gallup's StrengthsFinder's strengths. A StrengthsFinder is driven to see their future and map a path to it. However, most do not have this gene baked in and need assistance to being a part of it.

In fact, answering *positively* to the Seven Critical Needs should organically produce a development path and awareness of one's future. If team members understand and embrace the organization's core values and *why*; if they are accountable and embrace how they're measured; if they understand how their organization listens and how they are heard; then they should be able to develop the goals they need to work toward their imagined futures. Figuring out what's needed to achieve these goals to a large extent becomes the development program and requires a coach.

A coach has a natural desire to give of self for the benefit of another. A coach brings a methodical and consistent approach, so the effort is focused. Imagine using the Seven Critical Needs as a way to drive open and honest two-lives-working-on-one conversation to enable individuals to imagine their futures and map a path to it.

The coach who huddles with the team member can use the critical needs to ascertain the individual's long-term goals, help with strategies for getting there, and brainstorm tactics that will achieve the strategies. The tactics become more palatable when they're part of a courageous approach focused on a larger goal that might be one or several years out and is clearly aligned with the organization's *why*.

The coach and team are a catalyst or enabler, but the individual ideally does 80 percent of the work on development. Humans are more motivated when they have autonomy, and this is especially true of development. Also, on a practical level, leaders live in a core that might be several layers removed from the work various team members are doing. The individuals are the ones immersed in the work, perhaps four or five rings out. If we want them to own their roles, they must also own the procedures and processes that support them. Giving them the authority to refine those processes feeds development and underpins autonomy. The team member knows better than anyone where his or her gaps, talents, and potential paths forward lie. The role of your BOS is to codify and systemize how these development efforts happen and are maintained. It is not the sole domain of HR. Scaling Up/Rockefeller Habits has a tool they call their One-Page Personal Plan that is surrounded with development actions; EOS has a one-on-one meeting called the Quarterly Conversation where every 90 days' time is carved out to have an honest discussion around core values alignment, clarity on roles, and what the individual will make time to work on in the next 90 days, Rocks.

 ## Diagnosing How Much Work You Need to Do as an Organization

### • TO BE DEVELOPED •
*Exercise for PBOLTs and Senior Leadership to Answer*

Grab a piece of paper and follow these prompts.

1. What's the first word that comes to mind when someone says "development"?

2. Who is in charge of team members' development at your organization?

3. How often do leaders meet with team members to discuss their development?

4. Are development discussions baked into your *heard* conversations with commitments?

5. Is development tied to the skills required to fulfill roles?

After completing the prompts above, review your answers using my key below. Summarize how close your organization is to positive alignment on this critical need—and don't fudge. Remember, you're the one with the answers, and you probably know in your gut, without reading another word, how far you are from positive alignment. For each of your answers, give yourself a score from one of these four choices:

**WAY FAR | MANY MILES | RIGHT AROUND THE CORNER | THERE**

## Scoring Guide

**How to Score Prompt 1:** *What's the first word that comes to mind when someone says "development"?*

- If you answered "training," you're probably Way Far.

**How to Score Prompt 2:** *Who is in charge of team members' development at your organization?*

- If your answer was anything other than "team members," you're probably Way Far.

**How to Score Prompt 3:** *How often do leaders meet with team members to discuss their development?*

- If you answered more than 90 days, you're somewhere between Way Far and Right Around the Corner.
- If you said 90 days or less, you could be There or close to it.

**How to Score Prompt 4:** *Are development discussions baked into your heard conversations with employees, and is there a related plan the employee owns as part of their development?*

- If you answered yes to the discussion, but no to commitment, you are Right Around the Corner.
- If you said no, then you are Many Miles or Far Away.

**How to Score Prompt 5:** *Is development tied to the skills required to fulfill roles?*

- If you answered yes, then you are There or Right Around the Corner.
- If you answered no, then you are Way Far or Miles Away.

# CHAPTER 12

# To Be Balanced

<hr>

### Critical Need 7. To Be Balanced

**Organization Statement:** Our organization's definition of balance is clear and consistently communicated. We have work-life, compensation, and health and wellness mechanisms in place for people to participate in maintaining their own balance.

**Team Member/Individual Statement:** I understand and embrace my organization's definition of balance and the mechanisms I can participate in to reach my goal of balance. I understand that the three components of balance are (1) work-life, (2) compensation, (3) health and wellness. **I am balanced.**

<hr>

**THE TEAM MEMBER** who never takes time to recharge can begin to produce work that's as dull and meaningless as the sentence Jack

Nicholson typed over and over for hundreds of pages in that creepy old hotel: "All work and no play makes Jack a dull boy."

I saw this phenomenon in both team members and myself when I ran my own companies. When I left accounting to strike out on my own, I was very into bicycle racing, and one of my critical success factors was to train on my bike 150 days a year, so I could maintain my racing weight of 178 pounds. I did my best to make it, but when work got the better of me and I was sitting at my desk in midafternoon, my team would say, "Hey, Walt, have you ridden your bike yet today? Get out of here. You're making us nervous."

They knew that I would return refreshed and full of creative energy—and nearly always in a stellar mood. A bike ride was the break I needed for maximum creativity, but I'd had to skip it during the crazy audit seasons that dominate accounting. I had not yet fleshed out the Seven Critical Needs. Still, I knew on some level that I was not in positive alignment with the critical need *to belong* at my accounting job, so I self-selected out. I built a company where I could answer positively, and I tried to make sure that my team members could find balance too. If they needed a mental break to hit the gym, meditate, or whatever, that was fine with me as long as they cleared it with the team and didn't drop the ball on anything. Chief, a 10 AM person, was never awake before 9 AM. The team knew it, she knew it, the organization knew it. We and she belonged.

Balance exists in two realms for each of your people: workload and life load. Knowing where team members are in balance by taking a constant inventory is a key driver for courage. The two intersect in all sorts of ways. For instance, summers were busy at Layline, and the hours could be long, but our purpose and core values revolved around sailing, so it was understood that people would take off days, sometimes even a full week, to go to a regatta or participate on a sailboat racing team. We made sure that everyone knew when each person was taking off and that they covered for each other. The system was fair, honest, and clearly conveyed. Some balance issues stem from personality, or even nature, you might say. Chief absolutely brought it when she was awake. It took some time as a team to understand that this would not happen before 10 AM. As a team, we decided that she would start and leave later so that we could enjoy her at her fullest.

Chief was balanced, work was balanced, and SCARF needs were met. In all such instances, team members knew what was coming and who was covering for whom, so their sense of certainty, relatedness, and fairness was intact. The arrangement relied on autonomy, since people still had to take charge of their schedules and complete their projects, and those who pulled their weight tended to have a healthy status within the tribe. Like me after my bike rides, they also returned with heads clear and creative juices flowing. Their productivity was usually higher and recharged. They could engage in System 2 thinking.

Courage depends on the longevity and stamina of the team, and organizations that don't address balance head-on will never become courageously patient organizations. They tend to fall down here in the same ways they do on the rest of the Seven Critical Needs. The failures most often involve poor communication and a lack of empowerment.

First of all, balance is not only different for everyone; it's different for individual team members depending on the week, month, or year. There's the obvious stuff—a new baby, a sick parent, an illness—and lots that's less obvious: burnout, beloved hobbies, new domestic duties. A top-down, singular approach will achieve resentment, not balance, and it will SCARF people to no end. As with development, team members need to be empowered to take charge of their own balance, and that's only possible with good communication and a lack of fear.

Maintaining positive alignment to balance requires clarity, honesty, and regular communication, all functions of your BOS.

Questions about balance must be addressed at least—you guessed it—once a season, every 90 days at minimum. What's going on with team members outside of the organization? What's their outlook for the next 90 days, and what are leaders anticipating?

In what has become a famous story, Facebook COO Sheryl Sandberg asked some of the most powerful executives in the world at the World Economic Forum in Davos, Switzerland, how many had ever initiated a discussion about possible childbearing down the road with female employees. Not a single hand went up. The author of *Lean In: Women, Work, and the Will to Lead* wasn't surprised. HR departments tell you the topic is taboo, but her point was that such open discussions with valued team members could actually help women and their organizations plan better.

Of course we should respect privacy, but we have become too insistent that any and all personal information is off the table. It's often helpful to both the team member and the organization to have a conversation about what's going on in life that might affect work. Is your BOS facilitating this? Our go-to metaphor here is the sea mammal that returns to the depths refreshed, swimming and hunting better after it's had sufficient time to recharge, breathe $O_2$ on the surface. Team members need to be honest about how and why they want to recharge, take a break, get some space to think, breathe.

Organizations must be honest, too, and having policies and rules in place is no guarantee. Too many companies aren't clear about core values that mean working long hours as a deadline nears or a season gets in full swing. False advertising around balance expectations is one of the ways organizations wind up with team members who don't belong and who then spread dysfunction.

The last of the Seven Critical Needs about *balance* cycles back directly to the first, on *belonging*. I did not belong at EY when I became a CPA and took my first job, partly because I could never align to the firm's positive alignment regarding the subject of balance. The team members at the company I started, who were passionate about sailing and did belong, found a balance that for many was ideal.

Getting the balance right for myself and my team took courage. Figuring out workarounds because of illness, childbirth, or even simple mental breaks, requires courage. But positive alignment to balance returns that courage exponentially. It allows both team members and the organization to plan intelligently, think long-term, build stamina, and operate consistently, at full bore. As we have said, with courage comes consistency, with consistency comes stamina, and with stamina comes amazing repeatable results.

## Attaining and Maintaining Positive Alignment on Balance

We discussed balance mostly as a way to help people negotiate the demands of work and life. This is an important aspect of critical need seven, but not the only one. In a broader sense, balance also is about making sure team members have the most productive day possible. Part of that effort means making allowances for the demands of life outside of work, but it also involves carving out space and time for thought at work.

Keeping people chained to phones and emails every minute of the day can look highly productive at first glance, but in fact, it's a way to kill productivity. Especially in roles that require thinking and not just doing, team members need time to step back, rise above the daily work, and strategize. Leaders unwittingly encourage simplistic System 1 thinking with pressure or workloads so intense team members feel that they're living under constant threat, SCARFed on a daily basis. They don't have the time to pause in order to consider a better process or the flaws in a system if they're too entangled in it to see it clearly.

Organizations that neglect balance in this way create busy fools, always rushing from one fire to the next. The organization that helps team members to say "Positively, I have balance here" creates an environment that is proactive, not reactive. Allowing the space for balance, however, requires courage on the part of leaders. Most organizations see time as money, so letting people carve out time to just think, take time off for family issues, or allowing an hour for that important daily workout comes at a cost. Part of becoming a courageously patient organization is realizing that this cost pays high dividends in productivity, sharper System 2 thinking, anti-SCARF, and loyalty.

Most of the work of positive alignment on balance falls on the individual, around 90 percent. Only team members can fully appreciate the demands they're facing on and off the job, so it's up to them to bring up the issues, suggest what they need, and work at achieving balance.

## Promises Create Trust

When we promise our people compensation, safety, benefits, and work-life balance, it creates an expectation in them and holds us all accountable to our promises to do our jobs to fully execute the contract. In his book *The Morality of Freedom* and elsewhere, Joseph Raz advances a view that explicitly grounds the promissory power in our interests in self-binding for cooperation and coordination:

In the case of promises, the value of their power is that it expands people's ability to fashion their lives, or aspects of their lives, by their actions. "*Through their promises they commit themselves to others.* Decisions, as well as having goals, facilitate undertaking complex activities that require concerted actions. *Promises, being commitments to others, facilitate co-operation, the*

> *forging of relations that presuppose dependence, trust, and joint actions, and more."*
>
> Raz's observations point out something both obvious and essential to our critical needs framework: Promises, when kept, create trust. And trust is the fuel that powers belonging, buy-in, cooperation, collaboration, and great results. The flipside of the coin, of course, is that when promises are not kept, trust is destroyed. It takes a lot of kept promises to build up trust, but only one broken promise to destroy it. That puts a lot of pressure on promise makers to be promise keepers.

## Three Balance Influencers

Exactly like *development*, there are three areas that influence one's commitment to their own balance—again a triangulation: tribe, family, self, as we keep the ancestral metaphor moving.

Tribally, the organization must be very frank and clear about its work expectations. A CPA firm must be very clear that during busy season the firm will own you 80 hours per week. A retailer like Layline that has a busy season must be very clear that we do not think about leaving until the last customer is served and that we open on time.

As a team, "sharing the load" and "for the greater good" are the key terms here. A team needs to be aware of the talents and abilities of each teammate and help guide those unique abilities against the needs and priorities of the team. The team leader must demonstrate the four *A*s, not only in thinking about themselves but in helping the entire team be aligned, accountable, authentic, and aware as they orient to the overall good. When each team member views their own teammates as being AAAA, then open discussions around workload balance become natural and ongoing.

For the individual, the organization should make space for agreement and discussion around balance, ideally during a seasonal meeting with a coach. The priority for the coach is openness. *Here is what we are agreeing you're accountable for, here is how we are agreeing you will be measured. Are we in agreement?* I prefer "agreement" over "expectation" in this discussion because, as author Steve Chandler pointed out in a workshop I attended in Chicago years ago, expectations leave too much implied. They're one-sided, top down, and lead to disappointment. Agreement is fifty-fifty, with equal buy-in and commitment on both sides.

## Find Your Balance

Positive alignment on balance requires high levels of trust and honesty. If SCARF needs have been neglected, the kinds of conversations that help team members find balance become impossible. Working through the previous six critical needs is the best way to build trust and encourage honesty.

Here are some practical things to consider as team members work to get to positive alignment on balance. These should be driven by your BOS.

- **Belong and believe.** Is the balance between work and life that the organization allows honestly conveyed in its core values and *why*? If staying until the last customer is served or working 80-hour weeks at crunch time are vital to who you are, communicate that through core values, your *why*, policies, and your roles, so people can determine if your balance is right for them.
- **Open conversations.** It makes the HR department nervous, but during the seasonal meeting, ask team members about their lives and plans outside of work. If Pat is 32 and got

married three years ago, it's quite possible Pat is considering starting a family. Is that something Pat and the organization should plan for?

- **Check the diaper.** Nine out of ten times, a bad attitude, drop-off in productivity, or misalignment with core values is the result of some outside pressure, such as a sick child, a divorce, an alcohol addiction, or financial problems, for instance. For children, my mother-in-law would say: "Look to the physical first." This helps us remove the head trash around us thinking it is us. In other words, just be aware. What unpleasant stuff is someone carrying around that is making them unbalanced, miserable? Simply by paying attention, asking if something is wrong, asking what's going on, and letting a team member know that the organization cares, we create immense goodwill and, more importantly, an awareness of how we can reestablish balance. If we cannot see what is on the scale, it's impossible to balance that scale.

- **Accountability.** The assessment of all roles as part of getting to positive alignment on critical need three is a chance to restore balance for team members who might have found themselves helping out in areas not their own. Or perhaps they have found themselves occupying too many roles. Open conversations around this is the only way to find balance.

- **Communication.** Electronic interference in the form of endless emails, texts, and memos is frequently an obstacle to balance. I call this "our electronic leash." Going verbal can help address this. Off-site meetings, away from office distractions, will help leadership too. A former client of mine established the "no-email hour" from 10:45 to 11:45 every morning to boost focus and carve out space for higher-level thinking. We could call this the "courageous hour."

- **Policies.** It's important to be clear about the organization's policies on leave, sick days, and benefits. If they're on the books, they should be honored without hesitation. If a team member can't find balance within these parameters, he or she is at the wrong organization.
- **Leading.** Merely managing people destroys balance. Leading them with the four *A*s (alignment, accountability, authenticity, and awareness) and working for and maintaining positive alignment on the Seven Critical Needs provides the autonomy they desire. It's much easier for a team member who is being led and has autonomy to find balance.

 ## Diagnosing How Much Work You Need to Do as an Organization

### •TO BE BALANCED •

*Exercise for PBOLTs and Senior Leadership to Answer*

Grab a piece of paper and follow these prompts.

1. Find three random members of the team—one senior leader, one midlevel person, and someone on the front line—and ask, *On a scale of 1–10, how well are you able to balance work and life these days?*
2. Ask the same three team members to rate on a scale of 1–10 how well the organization understands and tries to help balance their life needs with work.
3. When is the last time you had a conversation with a team member about life outside of the organization and his or her needs in balancing it with work?

After completing the prompts above, review your answers using my key below. Summarize how close your organization is on this critical need—and don't fudge. Remember, you're the one with the answers, and you probably know in your gut, without reading another word, how far you are from *positive alignment*. For each of your responses, give yourself a score from one of these four choices:

**WAY FAR | MANY MILES | RIGHT AROUND THE CORNER | THERE**

*Scoring Guide*

**How to Score Prompt 1:** *Find three random members of the team— one senior leader, one midlevel person, and someone on the frontline— and ask, On a scale of 1–10, how well are you able to balance work and life these days?*

- If they answered from 7–10, you might be Right Around the Corner or even There.
- Less than 7 means you're somewhere between Way Far and Many Miles.

**How to Score Prompt 2:** *Ask the same three team members to rate on a scale of 1–10 how well the organization understands and tries to help balance their life needs with work.*

- If they answered from 7–10, you might be Right Around the Corner or even There. Less than 7 means you're somewhere between Way Far and Many Miles.

**How to Score Prompt 3:** *When is the last time you had a conversation with a team member about life outside of the organization and his or her needs in balancing it with work?*

- If you answered more than 90 days, you're Way Far. If you said 90 days or less, you might be Right Around the Corner or even There.

Before we dive into the conclusion, I want to point out something that probably occurred to you as you read about what the work organizations must do before any of their team members can get to positive alignment on the Seven Critical Needs:

It is often the organization's fault for not doing the work required to allow some to buy in. It may turn out, in fact, that those team members aren't troublemakers after all; they're just individual contributors whose company isn't courageous and patient enough to meet their SCARF and BITE needs. My grandfather liked to say, "If you go into town for a day, meet 100 people, and one of them acts like a horse's ass, then he's a horse's ass. If, on the other hand, you go into town and everyone you meet acts like a horse's ass, then *you're* a horse's ass." If your organization has too many jerks, then you bear much of the responsibility for creating an environment where BITE and SCARF needs aren't being met and folks can't possibly gain positive alignment to all of the Seven Critical Needs.

The good news? Hopefully you now have the perspective and tools you need to get the bad fits to buy in or select out. The first step: Can you get comfortable with a set of promises that sounds like this?

*Everyone, I am making a set of promises to you today. I plan to make and keep these promises in order to create one single organization where everyone belongs, believes, is accountable and measured, heard, developed, and balanced.*

- *When it comes to belonging, I promise to surround you with people who live into and through our core values and have or can develop the skills to do their job well.*

- *When it comes to believing, I promise to surround you with people who buy in to what we are doing, to what we are all about.*
- *When it comes to accountability, we want to get very clear about exactly how you contribute—what is the purpose of your job and the purpose of all the important roles you play. We want to get clear and maintain that clarity with you forever.*
- *When it comes to measured, we want to honor you with what makes a good job, we want to honor you with understanding why you are doing something so you can contribute your best efforts and know they are good efforts.*
- *When it comes to heard, we want to be very clear on when and how we listen. We will be very direct about how your opinion can be heard so you know you were heard. No, sorry, this does not mean we will take action on everything you say, but we will listen and communicate. We will close the loop.*
- *When it comes to developed, we will be very clear on how and when you can take control of your own development. This will be systematic and repeatable and will make sense to you.*
- *When it comes to balance, we will be very clear what our expectations for balance are, such as how much time a job should take for work-life balance, what the job pays, and how we might help you with physical balance.*

*In order to keep our promises, we will be using a business operating system called X. The rhythms and systems of X will ensure that you can stay positively aligned to these seven promises.*

# KEEP IT SIMPLE

**"I AM HELPING** *Sir Christopher Wren Build Saint Paul's Cathedral."*

Our mason with this simple response aligned positively to the Seven Critical Needs.

*"I am helping to put a man on the moon."*

Our NASA janitor with another simple response aligned positively to the seven.

It can be that simple.

How?

## Go Verbal, Make a Promise

**Go verbal** and make a promise to each person under your roof, to your organization as a whole:

> *Everyone, I am making a promise to you, we are going to build one single organization, a courageously patient organization. I am promising to surround you with these types of people. These are our core values. This is our* why. *I want you to be able to consider and positively align with these Seven Critical Needs, and here is how we go about that.*

A simple verbal promise is a very powerful thing and cannot be underestimated. A promise is a human psychological tool. When we say something in the form of a promise, it has a tendency to come true and we hold ourselves to a higher standard.

Most entrepreneurs have a dream before they have a business. I began this book by talking about that dream, the innovative product someone knew she could deliver, the smart organization someone was sure he could create, the superior service that would leave the competition stunned.

People were always at the center of that dream—smart and talented, sure, but more than that. The people you imagined when you set out to start an organization shared your core values, whether or not you called them that. They shared your purpose and were, quite simply, people you wanted to spend time with.

What happened? How did the people who don't really belong or believe creep in? Where did the daily dysfunction come from? Where did the dream go?

Don't worry; it's still there. Virtually all of your problems, as I've said throughout this book, are people problems, and the dream is alive and well. People are complex animals. If there's a gap between your original dream and the current organization, it likely exists because your systems for dealing with people—communicating with them, measuring them, managing and leading them—aren't adequate.

*Management* techniques never are. The headaches, dysfunction, and lack of focus you're facing are common. Management treats organizations and their members like soulless machines. It tends to ignore human psychology, social dynamics, even biology to impose order from on high. It is built according to profits and efficiency. We are all for both—they're the ultimate result of what we do—but the best way to address profits and efficiency, paradoxically, is to start with the needs of the human beings that make up the team, the organization.

What do the humans who are the organization want? (Remember, an organization is essentially a fiction that dies if enough people stop believing in it.) They want to be *led,* not managed. They want to belong and believe, to be truly accountable. They want to know that they are being measured fairly and that their opinions are heard. They want to develop and crave balance.

Becoming positively aligned to the Seven Critical Needs can resurrect and achieve the dream. There are only seven of them, and together, they cover all your team members' concerns, but as you know by now, getting to *yes* is tough. It takes time and effort, and if done correctly, it will inflict pain. The end of this book is just the beginning.

Don't panic. Panic is the opposite of courage, and courage is the goal here. Don't make this harder than it has to be. The Seven Critical Needs rest on common sense, and that should be your guide. Follow the steps we outlined for each need. For belonging, start by deciding on your core values and create a belief statement. *Go verbal* and make a promise to each person under your roof:

*We are trying to build a courageously patient organization. These are our core values. This is our why. We want you to be able to positively align with these Seven Critical Needs, and here is how we go about that.*

Lee Walker, the millennial CEO of Walker Auto & Truck, uses all of the models in BITE7. He acknowledges that this can seem complex, but moving a blue-collar team member who's never managed people into a leadership role—a common scenario for his business—is also complex. Walker has created a one-page handout that includes key elements of the Entrepreneurial Operating System (EOS) as well as the Seven Promises, highlighting the ways that culture, structure, and organizational operations overlap to facilitate strategic thinking.

"The challenge in an organization like ours is to make all this stuff accessible and not lose people in the discussion," Walker says.

"With these models, I can use one page to talk very simply about what we're doing to create structural clarity and what we are doing to build culture. What are we doing to create operational clarity and consistency, and what tools do we have in our toolbox? It's all there."

That single page, a great first step in making the organization visible, has become a powerful hiring tool, Walker says. He explains his handout and the company's core values during the first interview for management positions, when he does most of the talking. During a second interview, he looks for prospects who, though they don't yet understand all the terms, can demonstrate that they appreciate the concepts and want to contribute to an organization that believes in these things.

## Take Inventory of Your Business Operating System

The Seven Critical Need Statements themselves are the best for this purpose and will help you assess whether or not your current business operating system is adequate. A good BOS should get positive alignment on all seven needs. Some are quite good overall but leave gaps in certain areas. The gaps must be patched or the organization suffers. If you developed a BOS yourself, organically, does it get you to *yes* on the Seven Questions? If so, they can be overlaid seamlessly onto your BOS to build courage in the organization. If not, the seven will highlight where your operating system is falling short. Can it be improved, or should you consider installing a prepackaged BOS?

Any BOS can be customized to fit your organization—that's the whole idea—and the pace will also vary, depending on the facts on the ground. Some leaders can honestly say, *yes, we are two years into a core values initiative, and we have thought deeply about our purpose.* They might need work on accountability and measurement, say, but be close to *yes* in most areas. Others perhaps have never thought seriously about incorporating core values into the organization and face a longer road.

After you have analyzed your BOS fit to the seven, think of the tools you must develop and include in your BOS to get the team to positive alignment. How will you structure your seasonal meeting? What will your rubrics look like? There is no need to reinvent the wheel here. Visit our website—www.BITE7.com—and you will find an inventory of links to tools from various BOSs and thinkers that you can use as part of your BOS.

## Be Courageous: Make and Keep Your Promises

Whatever your status, transformation does not happen quickly. A strong effort, in our experience, takes 18 months to bear fruit and three years to fully implement. The effort doesn't end in three years, of course. In a sense, it never ends. The organization is always striving to get people to positive alignment and to maintain it, to keep filling the buckets that turn the waterwheel and drive the courageously patient organization.

As you work through the seven, however, and begin getting to positive alignment, you'll feel momentum growing. There are two sides to this lens. As the organization looks through one and tries to answer *yes*, the individual is gazing through the other to do the same. Team members will shoulder much of the burden if they're led rather than managed. Because the organization is granting them more autonomy and working to meet their needs, they won't even see it as a burden—more like a liberating force.

For now, forget about the theory we explored earlier and the more complex pieces of the puzzle. The difficult bits will come in time, and the theory can be skipped entirely if you don't care what's under the hood. Much of my excitement at discovering the Seven Critical Needs and Promises had to do with their simplicity. Here are seven basic things every team member and leader can remember and appreciate. Keep it simple.

These are our values. This is our purpose. Can you say *yes*?

Yes, I belong.

Yes, I believe.

Yes, I understand and embrace how I am accountable.

Yes, I understand and embrace how I am measured.

Yes, I understand and embrace how I am heard.

Yes, I understand and embrace how I am developed.

Yes, I understand and embrace how I am balanced.

This can be as simple as just having a seasonal conversation with each individual. If you open the door, they will take the lead and do the heavy lifting.

Final advice.

If you feel like you have made it complex, you have.

Simplify, focus, say *no*. Be ruthlessly courageous as you attract and repel.

Love,

# ACKNOWLEDGMENTS

*Life:*

Walter L. Brown Jr., Tom Gower, Carl Hudson, Ron Scheeler, Tee-Wee Blount, Dr. Robert White, Dr. Randy White, Dr. Junius H. Terrell, Olaf and Peter Harken, Paul McKee, Alistair Murray, Bob Bitchin

*As a Direct Influence on this Book:*

Greg Walker, Don Tinney, Gino Wickman, Dan Sullivan, Patrick Lencioni, Brené Brown, Dr. Dino Signore, Dr. Jim Clifton, Dr. John Grinnell, Steven Covey, Bulldog (Jonathan Smith), Wildstyle (Jill Walker), Clearman (Greg Cleary), MOD (Mark O'Donnell), Shrek (Chris White), Tom Bouwer, David Rock, Clay Gilbert, Alex Freytag, Marion Brown, Jane Brown, Rock (Duane Marshall), Hurricane (Ken Dewitt), Barry Pearce, Allen Cobb, Chris Dawson, and to all the teams who have traveled with me to BITE.

# ADDITIONAL RESOURCES AND TOOLS

### Tool: Seven Question Bite Survey

The BITE Survey is a short survey that walks team members through the Seven Critical Needs, asking them to rate each on a simple 1–10 scale. This is the way we kick off the initiative with team members, gauge how much work lies ahead, and begin forming a strategy.

This survey has been scaled to fit this book from its original 8.5 x 11-inch size. If you'd like to print out your own copy, you can find the survey at Bite7.com.

# SEVEN QUESTION BITE SURVEY™

**For each of the 7 questions,** you will be asked to consider **several critical factors.** Take a little time to think about each, determine which factors are most important to you, then come up with a score. Don't stress out. **Trust your gut feeling.** Scores are mandatory for each question. Written feedback is optional, but **we strongly encourage you to explain your scores.** Your explanations are what allow us to have the clearest idea of what's working and not working so that we can come up with a tailored plan to make the organization stronger and your work experience better.

**Instructions:**

- A score of **1** means you are answering the question with the strongest "**No!**" possible.
- A score of **10** means you are answering the question with the strongest "**Yes!**" possible.

| 1 = NO, NOT AT ALL | | | | | | | | 10 = YES, ABSOLUTELY | |
|---|---|---|---|---|---|---|---|---|---|

### DO I BELONG?
*I understand and embrace my organization's core values, and I have (or can develop) the skills my job demands.* ***I belong.***

| 1 | 2 | 3 | 4 | 5 | 6 | 7 | 8 | 9 | 10 |
|---|---|---|---|---|---|---|---|---|---|

COMMENTS:

### DO I BELIEVE?
*I know and believe in my organization's Why. I also believe in our leadership, my teammates, our strategic direction, and the products or services we provide.* ***I believe.***

| 1 | 2 | 3 | 4 | 5 | 6 | 7 | 8 | 9 | 10 |
|---|---|---|---|---|---|---|---|---|---|

COMMENTS:

### DO I UNDERSTAND AND EMBRACE WHAT I'M ACCOUNTABLE FOR?
*I understand and embrace the purpose of my job and the roles that make up my job. I know what I should be thinking about and doing and why.* ***I am accountable.***

| 1 | 2 | 3 | 4 | 5 | 6 | 7 | 8 | 9 | 10 |
|---|---|---|---|---|---|---|---|---|---|

COMMENTS:

### DO I UNDERSTAND AND EMBRACE HOW I'M MEASURED?
*I understand and embrace how and why I am measured, and I know what constitutes a "good job." My measures give me direction and help me form strategies to do great work in all of my roles.* ***I am well measured.***

| 1 | 2 | 3 | 4 | 5 | 6 | 7 | 8 | 9 | 10 |
|---|---|---|---|---|---|---|---|---|---|

COMMENTS:

### DO I UNDERSTAND AND EMBRACE HOW I'M HEARD?
*I understand and embrace how and when my organization listens and responds.* ***I am heard.***

| 1 | 2 | 3 | 4 | 5 | 6 | 7 | 8 | 9 | 10 |
|---|---|---|---|---|---|---|---|---|---|

COMMENTS:

### DO I UNDERSTAND AND EMBRACE HOW I'M DEVELOPED?
*I understand and embrace my organization's development mechanisms and how I can develop; I know how to take an active role in my own development.* ***I am developing.***

| 1 | 2 | 3 | 4 | 5 | 6 | 7 | 8 | 9 | 10 |
|---|---|---|---|---|---|---|---|---|---|

COMMENTS:

### DO I UNDERSTAND AND EMBRACE HOW I MAINTAIN BALANCE?
*I understand and embrace my organization's definition of balance and the mechanisms I can use to reach my goals for balance. (Three components of balance: 1. Work-life, 2. Compensation, 3. Health and Wellness.)* ***I am balanced.***

| 1 | 2 | 3 | 4 | 5 | 6 | 7 | 8 | 9 | 10 |
|---|---|---|---|---|---|---|---|---|---|

COMMENTS:

**BITE7™**
BUY-IN | INCLUSION | TRUST | ENGAGEMENT

**WWW.BITE7.COM**
© 2018-2024 7Q7P, LLC. All Rights Reserved.

## Tool: The BITE Index Report

### Measure your Organization's Health

**How effective is your BOS Installation?**
The BITE Index is a measure of your organizational health and tells you how well you and your BOS are doing at meeting the Seven Critical Needs and keeping your Seven Promises. Your BITE Index Report will include a summary page like the one below along with pages that dive into each critical need. It includes anonymous comments that are tied to each critical need along with the score the individual who is commenting gave for that need. The report can be sorted by manager, location, etc. All the feedback you need to formulate your action plan is included in the report; it is a multiple-page report that includes your BITE scores and feedback tied to each critical need.

# BITE7™ Report

| Average | Question | Index |
|---------|----------|-------|
| 9.30 | I Belong | 78 |
| 8.93 | I Believe | 61 |
| 9.26 | I'm Accountable | 74 |
| 8.80 | I'm Measured | 54 |
| 8.70 | I'm Heard | 54 |
| 9.02 | I'm Developed | 67 |
| 8.67 | I'm Balanced | 50 |

| BITE7 INDEX™: | 63 |
|---------------|-----|

*Buy-in, Inclusion, Trust, Engagement*

**BITE7 INDEX™ Key**

| -100 to 50 = Weak | 51 to 69 = Average | 70+ = Strong |
|-------------------|--------------------|--------------|

| 🏚 DISENGAGED | 😐 NEUTRAL | 🔋 ENGAGED |
|---------------|-----------|-----------|
| 15 | 90 | 217 |
| 5% | 28% | 67% |

| Total Respondents | 46 |
|-------------------|-----|
| Total Responses | 322 |
| Average | 8.96 |
| Report Date | 6/23/2023 |

*The summary page of the Bite Index Report*

## Tool: The BITE Mapping Guide

### *Map the tools of your BOS to the Seven Critical Needs*

Here you will find examples of the BITE Mapping Guide tool we share with clients. Ask yourself: Does the tool from our BOS help or enable a person to achieve positive alignment to the critical need? If it does, it receives a check mark; if not, it is left blank. When adding a new BOS tool, you can use the matrix to determine if one tool option covers more critical need bases than another.

# Example: EOS Tools to the Seven Critical Needs

# BITE MAPPING GUIDE
**FOR COMPANIES RUNNING ON EOS®**

| Your Business Operating System Tools | Belong | Believe | Accountable | Measured | Heard | Developed | Balanced |
|---|:---:|:---:|:---:|:---:|:---:|:---:|:---:|
| V/TO™ | ✔ | ✔ | | | | ✔ | |
| CORE VALUES | ✔ | | ✔ | | | | |
| ACCOUNTABILITY CHART™ | ✔ | | | ✔ | | ✔ | |
| GWC™ | ✔ | | ✔ | | ✔ | ✔ | ✔ |
| PEOPLE ANALYZER™ | ✔ | | ✔ | | ✔ | ✔ | |
| SCORECARDS | | ✔ | ✔ | ✔ | ✔ | ✔ | |
| ROCKS | | ✔ | ✔ | ✔ | ✔ | ✔ | |
| MEETING PULSE™ | | | | | ✔ | ✔ | |
| LEVEL 10 MEETING™ | | | | | ✔ | ✔ | |
| IDS™ | | ✔ | | | ✔ | ✔ | |
| 5-5-5™ | ✔ | ✔ | ✔ | ✔ | ✔ | ✔ | ✔ |
| LMA™ | | | | | ✔ | ✔ | ✔ |
| | | | | | | | |
| | | | | | | | |
| | | | | | | | |
| | | | | | | | |

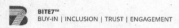

**BITE7™**
BUY-IN | INCLUSION | TRUST | ENGAGEMENT

# BITE MAPPING GUIDE

FOR COMPANIES RUNNING ON SCALING UP / GAZELLES

| Your Business Operating System Tools | Belong | Believe | Accountable | Measured | Heard | Developed | Balanced |
|---|---|---|---|---|---|---|---|
| OPPP (One Page Personal Plan) | | | | | ✔ | ✔ | ✔ |
| FACe (Functional Accountability Chart) | | | ✔ | ✔ | | | |
| PACe (Process Accountability Chart) | | | ✔ | ✔ | | | |
| SWT (SWOT) | | ✔ | | | | | |
| 7 Strata | | ✔ | | | | | |
| One Page Strategic Plan | ✔ | ✔ | ✔ | | | | |
| Vision Summary | ✔ | ✔ | ✔ | | | | |
| Who What When (WWW) | | ✔ | ✔ | ✔ | | | |
| Rockefeller Habits Checklist | ✔ | ✔ | ✔ | ✔ | ✔ | | |
| Cash Acceleration Strategies | | ✔ | | | | | |
| The Power of One | | ✔ | ✔ | ✔ | | | |
| | | | | | | | |
| | | | | | | | |
| | | | | | | | |
| | | | | | | | |
| | | | | | | | |

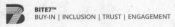

# BITE MAPPING GUIDE
## FOR COMPANIES RUNNING ON OTHER BUSINESS OPERATING SYSTEMS

| Your Business Operating System Tools | Belong | Believe | Accountable | Measured | Heard | Developed | Balanced |
|---|---|---|---|---|---|---|---|
| | | | | | | | |
| | | | | | | | |
| | | | | | | | |
| | | | | | | | |
| | | | | | | | |
| | | | | | | | |
| | | | | | | | |
| | | | | | | | |
| | | | | | | | |
| | | | | | | | |
| | | | | | | | |
| | | | | | | | |
| | | | | | | | |
| | | | | | | | |
| | | | | | | | |
| | | | | | | | |

## Additional Resources: Help and Information

Our goal is for you to magnetize your company so you are always attracting the right people and repelling the wrong ones on your way to creating and maintaining the culture you always dreamed of.

**The BITE7 Proven Process**—The following image represents the steps we take clients through to implement and master the BITE7 Framework. You can self-implement the BITE7 Framework or you can engage a BITE7 coach who will guide you through the entire BITE7 Proven Process represented below.

# THE BITE7 PROVEN PROCESS™

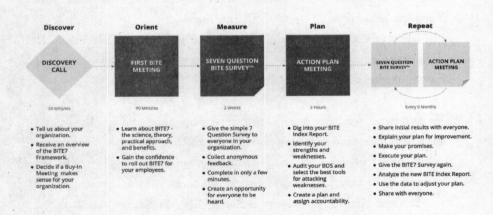

**BITE7.com** is our home website, which you might want to check out.

## Additional Resource: Using BITE7 as Your BOS Roll-Out Platform

*Using the seven to introduce, roll out, and monitor the effectiveness of your BOS implementation*

BOS implementations fail or get stuck for three reasons: (1) Employees do not understand the *why*; they cannot see what's in it for me (them), WIIFM. (2) Employees see the BOS as being done *to* them and not *for* them. (3) Employees do not see how management is going to stay committed to the effort via measurement and communication.

Leveraging the seven to introduce your BOS efforts, explain the *why*, and flip the script will empower employees to see you doing this for them and not to them. Rolling a BOS is a never-ending process, new people are joining your firm all the time, and your people need a regular reminder. Your rollout approach is a simple, repeatable, and complete process with the BITE7 Framework.

Most of my clients officially introduce and roll out EOS at their first State of the Company meeting immediately following their first Quarterly.

By this time, we have been together working and practicing for 150 days, and the team has been sharing the EOS tools inside their organization as they felt comfortable. There is no precise timing of when to use a BOS tool, and each situation warrants its own application.

Rollout timing: In Vision Building Day 2, clients take a Rock to engage with a BITE7 Concierge Coach to take them through the BITE7 Proven Process. This sets them up with a BITE Survey account and takes them through the 90-Minute Orientation Meeting.

After the 90-Minute Orientation Meeting, we help them administer their first BITE Survey and get their first BITE Index Report so they are ready for their first Quarterly off-site. In the first Quarterly off-site, as an EOS Implementer, I teach the EOS tool LMA. LMA is the final foundational tools we need to have an understanding of order to make and keep our Seven Promises. (See the EOS Tools to Seven Critical Needs matrix previously shown.)

Using the results from the BITE Survey reflected in the BITE Index, the team processes "roll out" as an issue in this Quarterly and decides on timing and takes a Roll-out Rock. The Rock normally includes the Action Plan Meeting with their BITE7 Concierge Coach and finalizes the roll-out agenda and script.

# BIBLIOGRAPHY

Adkins, Amy. "Employee Engagement in U.S. Stagnant in 2015." Gallup.com, Apr. 19, 2023. http://news.gallup.com/poll/188144 /employee-%20engagement-stagnant-2015.aspx.

Aquinas, Thomas. *The Summa Theologica of St. Thomas Aquinas, Translated by English Dominicans*. London: Burns, Oates, and Washbourne. Reprinted in New York: Christian Classics, 1981.

Atkins, Andy. "Building Workplace Trust: Trends and High Performance." Interaction Associates, Inc., 2014.

Brown, Brené. *Dare to Lead: Brave Work, Tough Conversations, Whole Hearts*. New York: Random House, 2018.

Chandler, Steve. "Choices for a More Powerful You." SteveChandler .com. https://www.stevechandler.com/choices.html.

Covey, Stephen. *Speed of Trust: The One Thing That Changes Everything*. New York: Simon & Schuster, 2008.

Covey, Stephen M. R., and Douglas R. Conant. "The Connection Between Employee Trust and Financial Performance." *Harvard Business Review*, Aug. 31, 2021. https://hbr.org/2016/07/the -connection-between-employee-trust-and-financial-performance.

Darwall, Stephen. *The Second Person Standpoint: Morality, Respect, and Accountability*. Cambridge, MA: Harvard University Press, 2006.

Delzonnia, Laura. "High Performing Teams Need Psychological Safety." *Harvard Business Review*, Aug. 24, 2017. https://hbr .org/2017/08/high-performing-teams-need-psychological-safety -heres-how-to-create-it.

Duhigg, Charles. "What Google Learned from Its Quest to Build the Perfect Team." *New York Times Magazine*, Feb. 25, 2016. https:// www.nytimes.com/2016/02/28/magazine/what-google-learned -from-its-quest-to-build-the-perfect-team.html.

Edmondson, Amy. "Psychological Safety and Learning Behavior in Work Teams." *Administrative Science Quarterly* 44, no. 2 (1999): 350–383. https://doi.org/10.2307/2666999.

Freytag, Alex, and Tom Bouwer. *Profit Works: Unravel the Complexity of Incentive Plans to Increase Employee Productivity, Cultivate an Engaged Workforce, and Maximize Your Company's Potential.* Powell, OH: Author Academy Elite, 2020.

Gallup. "The Benefits of Employee Engagement." Gallup.com, January 7, 2023. https://www.gallup.com/workplace/236927/employee -engagement-drives-growth.aspx.

Gallup. "How Millennials Want to Work and Live." 2016. https:// enviableworkplace.com/wp-content/uploads/Gallup-How -Millennials-Want-To-Work.pdf.

Gallup. "State of the Global Workplace Report." Gallup.com, June 30, 2023. http://www.gallup.com/workplace/349484/state-of-the -global-workplace.aspx.

Gerber, Michael. *The E-Myth: Why Most Businesses Don't Work and What to Do About It*, 2nd ed. Pensacola, FL: Ballinger Publishing, 2004.

Grinnell, John. *Beyond Belief: Awaken Potential, Focus Leadership.* Seattle, WA: Promethean-Mind Media, 2014.

Habib, Allen. "Promises to the Self." *Canadian Journal of Philosophy*, 39, no. 4 (2009): 537–558. https://doi.org/10.1353/cjp.0.0061.

Habib, Allen. "Promises." *Stanford Encyclopedia of Philosophy* (Winter 2022 Edition), Edward N. Zalta & Uri Nodelman (eds.). https://plato.stanford.edu/archives/win2022/entries/promises/.

Harari, Yuval Noah. *Homo Deus: A Brief History of Tomorrow*. New York: HarperCollins, 2017.

Hare, R. M. "The Promising Game," *Revue Internationale de Philosophie*, 18(70): 398–412. Reprinted in *The Is-Ought Question: A Collection of Papers on the Central Problems in Moral Philosophy*, W. D. Hudson (ed.). London: Macmillan, 1969: 144–156.

Harnish, Verne. *Mastering the Rockefeller Habits: What You Must Do to Increase the Value of Your Growing Firm*. Ashburn, VA: Gazelles Inc., 2002.

Harnish, Vern. *Scaling Up: How a Few Companies Make It . . . and Why the Rest Don't*. Ashburn, VA: Gazelles Inc., 2014.

Hart, H. L. "Are There Any Natural Rights?" *Philosophical Review*, 64, no. 2 (1955): 175. https://doi.org/10.2307/2182586.

Hume, David A. *A Treatise of Human Nature*. Reprinted, L. A. Selby-Bigge (ed.), London: Oxford University Press, 1896. Second edition revised by P. H. Nidditch, Oxford: Clarendon Press, 1975.

Kahneman, Daniel. *Thinking, Fast and Slow*. London: Penguin Books, 2011.

Lencioni, Patrick M. *The Five Dysfunctions of a Team: A Leadership Fable*. Hoboken, NJ: Jossey-Bass, 2002.

Lencioni, Patrick M. "Make Your Values Mean Something." *Harvard Business Review*, July 2002. https://hbr.org/2002/07/make-your-values-mean-something.

Lencioni, Patrick M. *The Truth About Employee Engagement: A Fable About Addressing the Three Root Causes of Job Misery*. Hoboken, NJ: Jossey-Boss, 2015.

Osinga, Frans. *Science, Strategy and War: The Strategic Theory of John Boyd*. Abington, UK: Routledge, 2006.

Owens, David. "A Simple Theory of Promising." *Philosophical Review*, 115, no. 1 (2006): 51–77. https://doi.org/10.1215/00318108-2005 -002.

Raz, Joseph. *The Morality of Freedom*. Oxford: Oxford University Press, 1986.

Re, Daniel E., and Nicholas O. Rule. "Predicting Firm Success from the Facial Appearance of Chief Executive Officers of Non-Profit Organizations." *Perception*, 45, no. 10 (October 2016): 1137–1150. https://doi.org/10.1177/0301006616652043.

Rigoni, Brandon, and Bailey Nelson. "Few Millennials Are Engaged at Work." Gallup.com, May 5, 2023. http://news.gallup.com /businessjournal/195209/few-millennials-engaged-work.aspx.

Rigoni, Brandon, and Bailey Nelson. "Millennials Not Connecting with Their Company's Mission." Gallup.com, Nov. 15, 2016. http://news.gallup.com/businessjournal/197486/millennials-not-connecting-company-mission.aspx.

Robertson, Brian J. *Holacracy: The New Management System for a Rapidly Changing World*. New York: Henry Holt and Company, 2015.

Rock, David. "Managing with the Brain in Mind." strategy+business, Aug. 27, 2009. https://www.strategy-business.com/article/09306.

Shiffrin, Seana Valentine. "The Divergence of Contract and Promise." *Harvard Law Review*, 120, no. 3 (2007): 709–749.

Sinek, Simon. "How Great Leaders Inspire Action." Filmed September 2009 at TEDxPuget, Newcastle, WY. Video. 17:58. https://www .ted.com/talks/simon_sinek_how_great_leaders_inspire_action.

Sullivan, Dan. *How the Best Get Better*. Toronto: Strategic Coach Inc., 2001.

Wickman, Gino. *Traction: Get a Grip on Your Business*. Dallas, TX: BenBella Books, 2012.

# ABOUT THE AUTHOR

Walt Brown (he/him) has always been a team guy. He is a student of and active player/coach of Organizational Health.

Winning as a team is a core part of Walt's life, and this team passion coupled with sets and reps of experience has molded his understanding that winning in business is all about the entire organization as a team.

This philosophy is shaped most recently through his coaching and consulting practice, where he has facilitated more than 1,500 full-day senior leadership team off-site sessions across more than 200 companies doing the gutsy work of working on their business.

Prior to his coaching and consulting life, Walt ran on a track made up of two parallel team rails. On one rail were the four team-based companies he founded and ran from the age of 24 until his exit at 46.

On the other rail was a life of world-class competitive sailboat racing on boats that had teams, 7 to 17 crew each. For 30 years he raced an average of 78 days a year in places like Key West, Newport, San Francisco, Antigua, St. Martin, and Sardinia.

He is working on a fourth book, tentatively titled *Seeing the Invisible: Two Strategic Thinking Models to Empower Your People*. The book features interviews with international business moguls who are also active sailboat racers/round-the-world sailors. In the interviews they reflect on the overlap of competitive sailboat racing, business, and strategy.

Walt lives in North Carolina with his wife of 39 years. He has two adult daughters and a recent granddaughter. He has retired from sailing. His winter passion is powder skiing in Alta, Utah; he is deeply involved in beaver habitat conservation; and weekly he rides mountain bikes with his trail-dog, a standard poodle, named Buddy Holly, who has his own YouTube channel @buddyhollytrailpoodle2064.

Visit Walt online at https://waltbrown.co.